Vincent van Gogh Starry Night Dreamer

by
Alesandra Weekley

Vincent van Gogh Starry Night Dreamer

by Alesandra Weekley

Illustrated by Jordan Weekley, David Weekley

© 2018 David & Alesandra Weekley

All rights reserved.

Note: Adjustments were made to Vincent van Gogh's paintings for the purposes of this book

Vincent van Gogh once said
I dream my paintings
then I paint my dreams

This book is dedicated
to all the little dreamers and artist out there

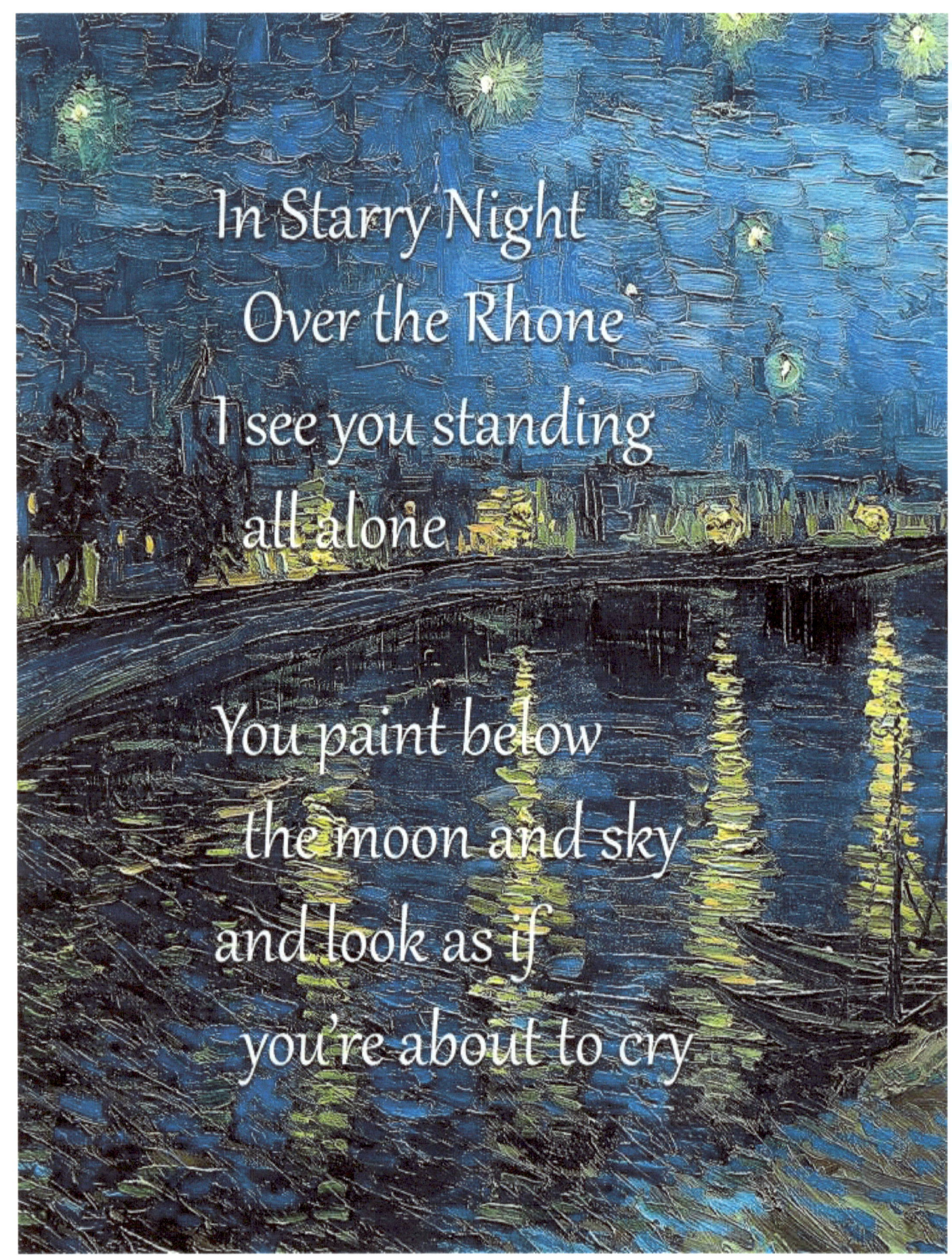

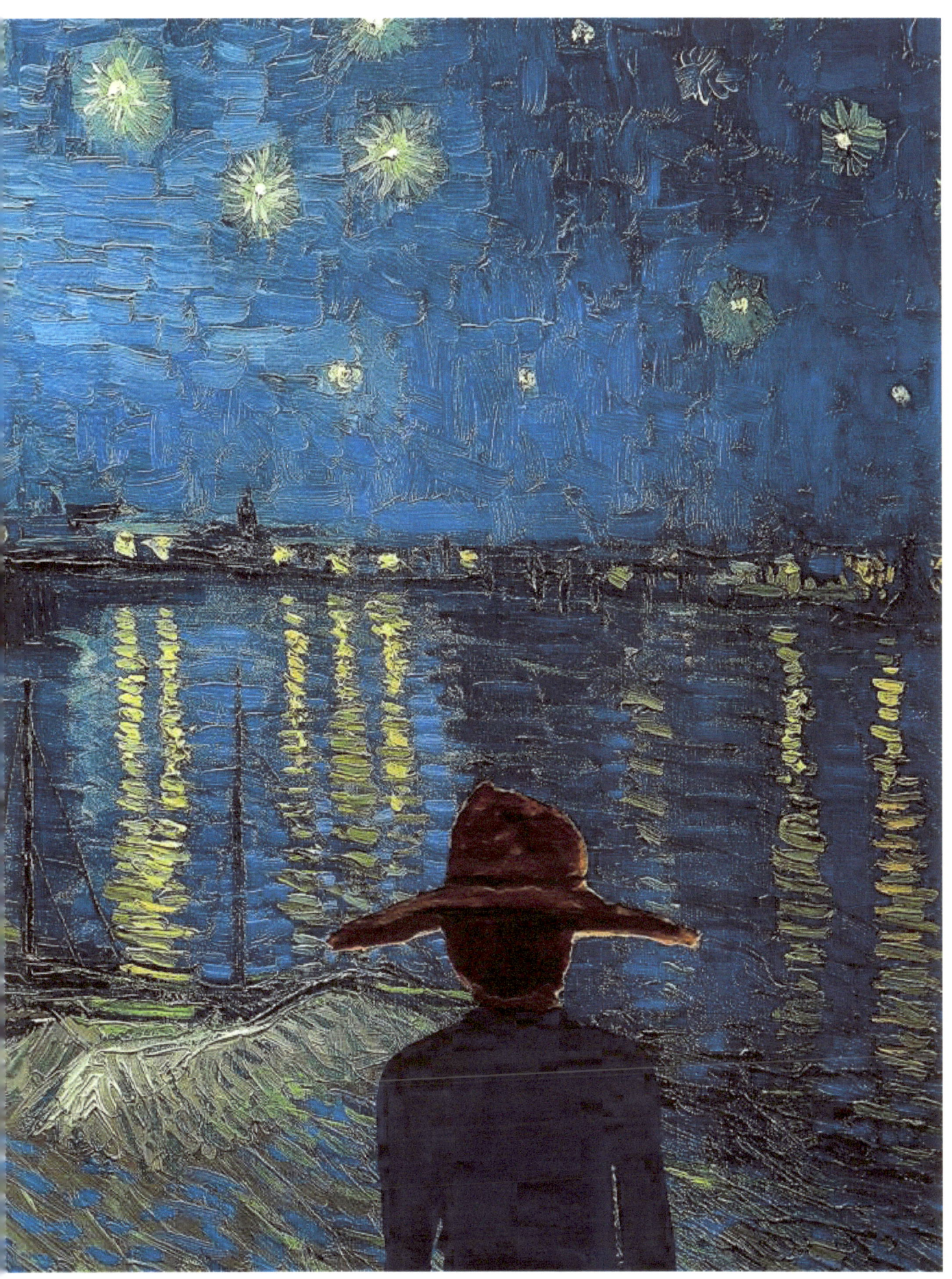

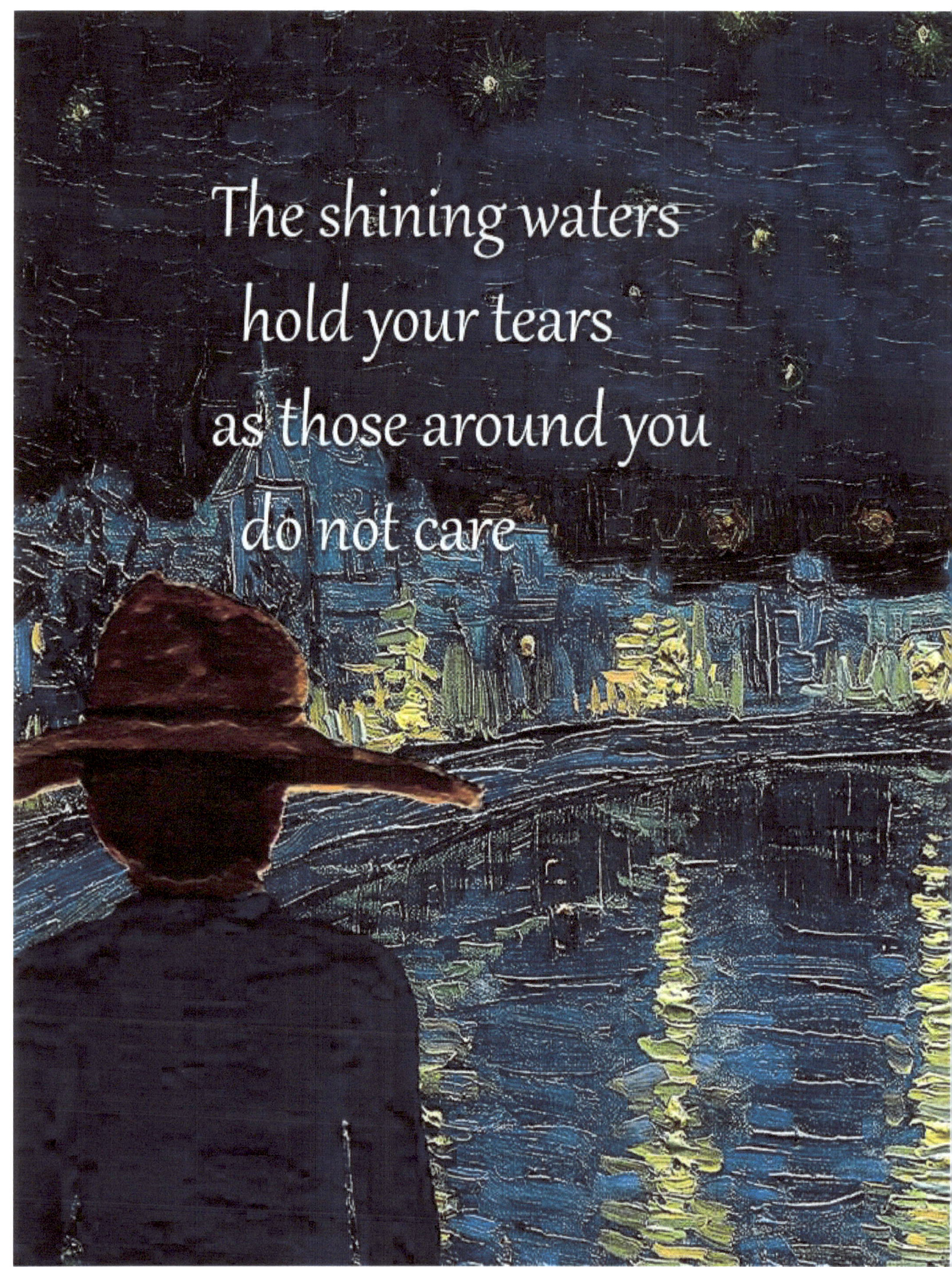

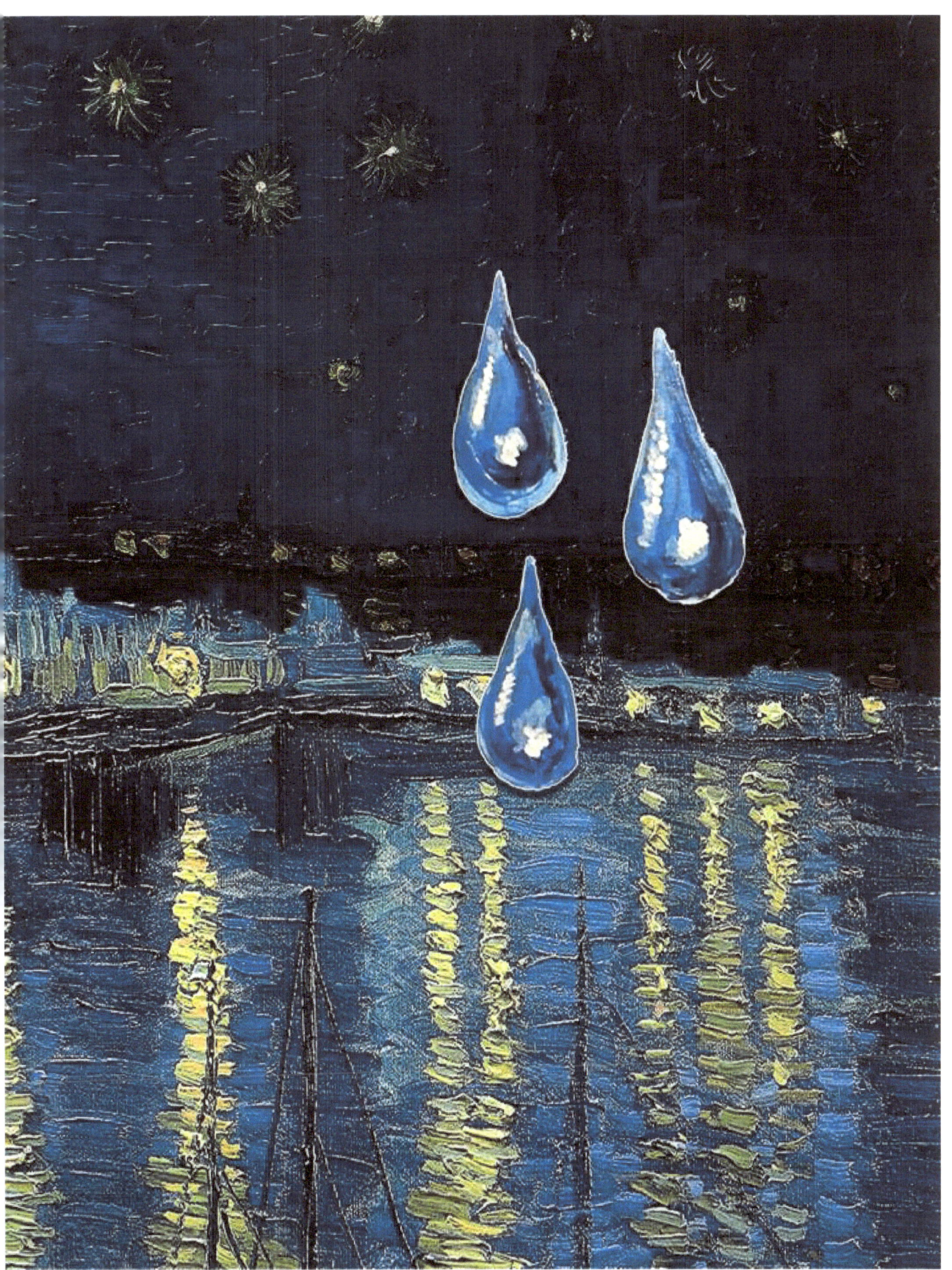

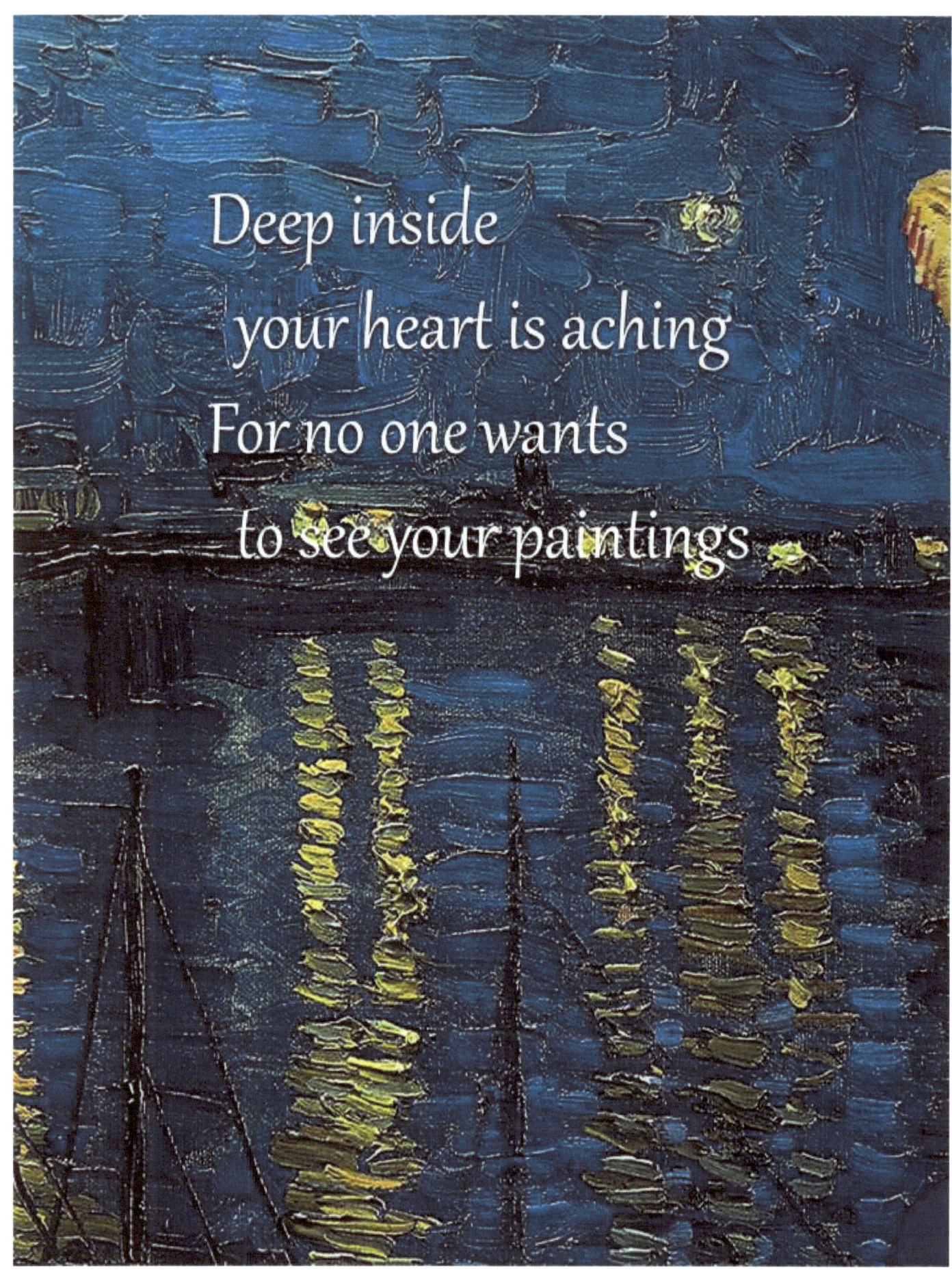

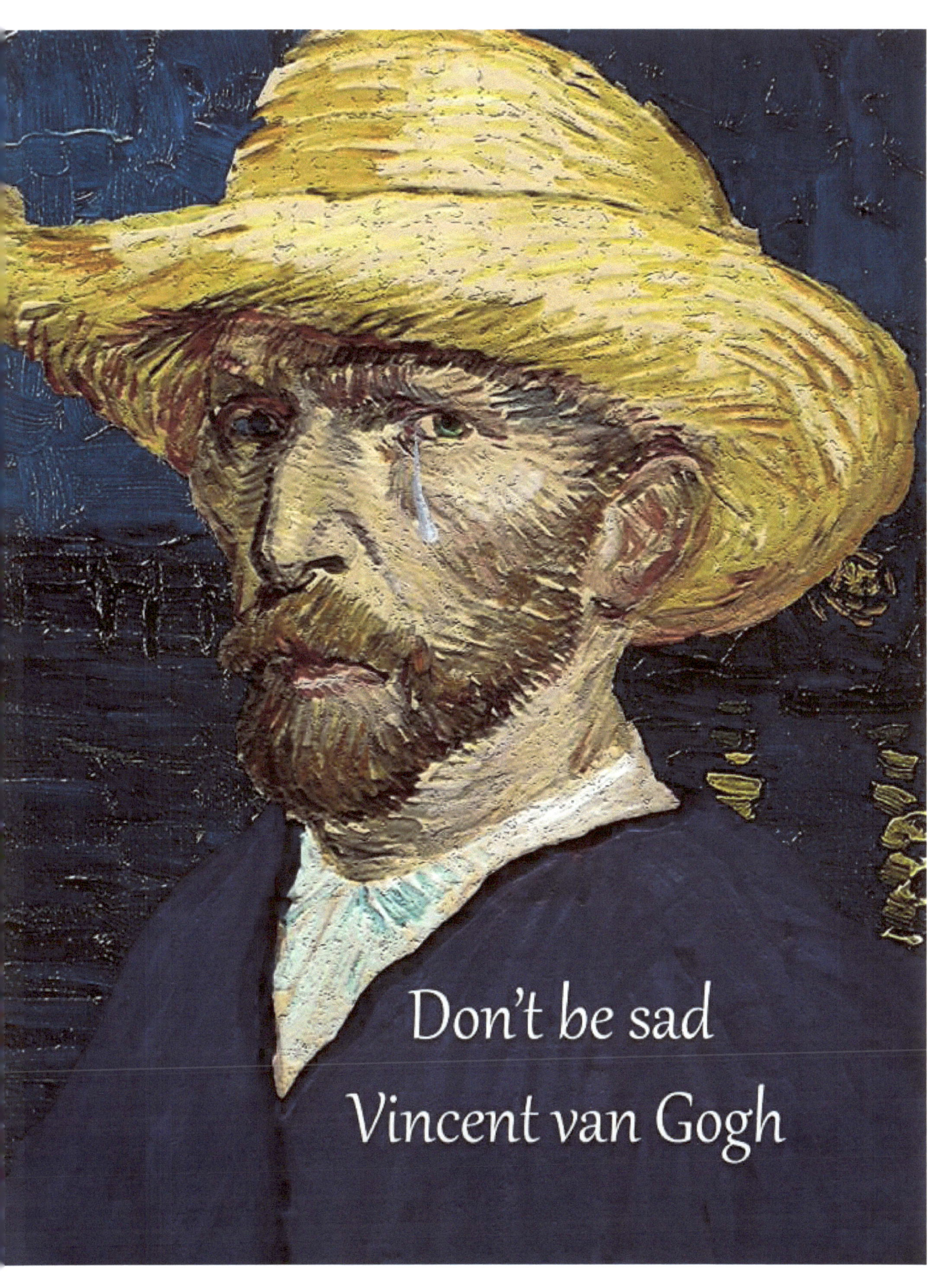

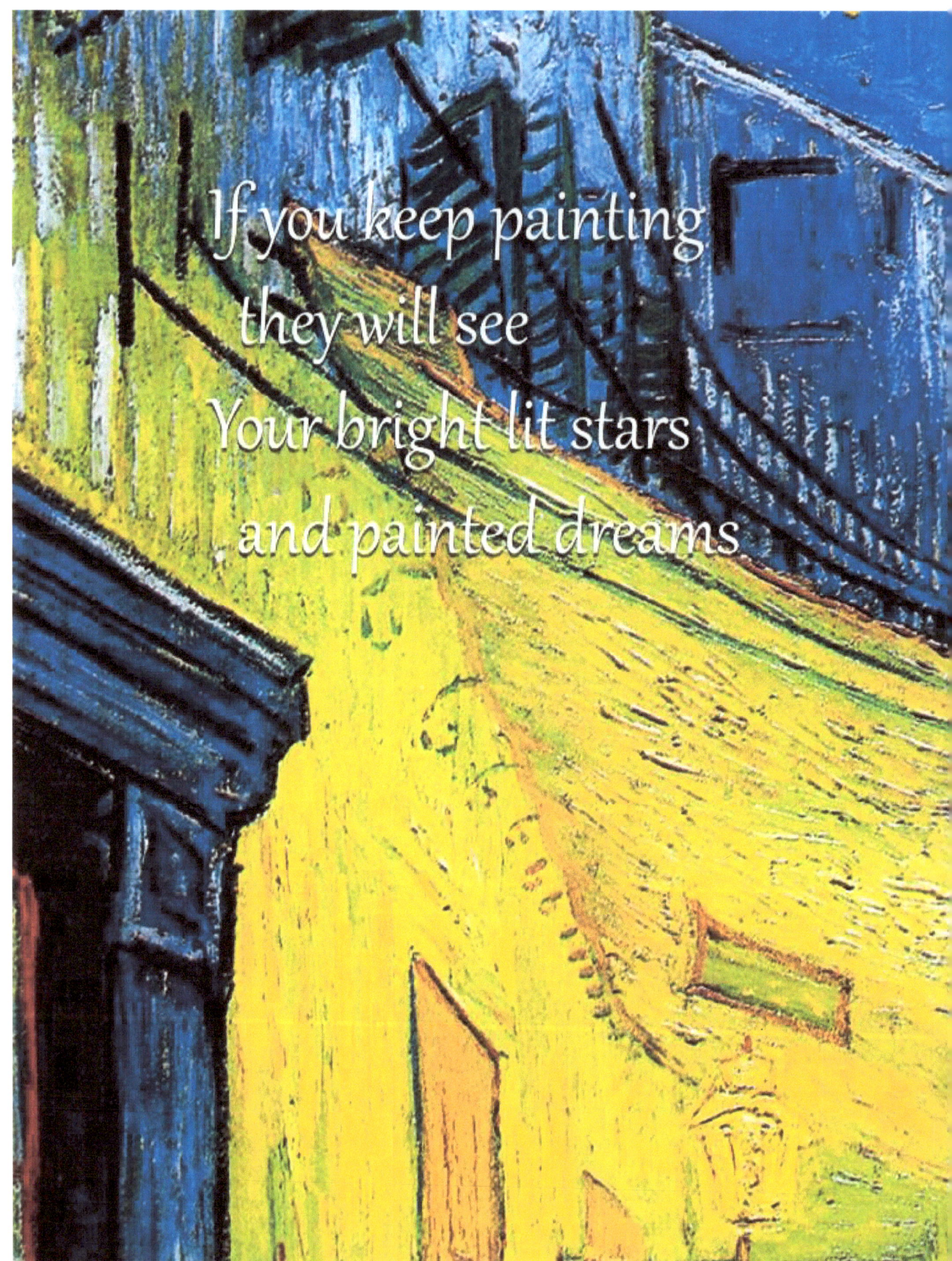

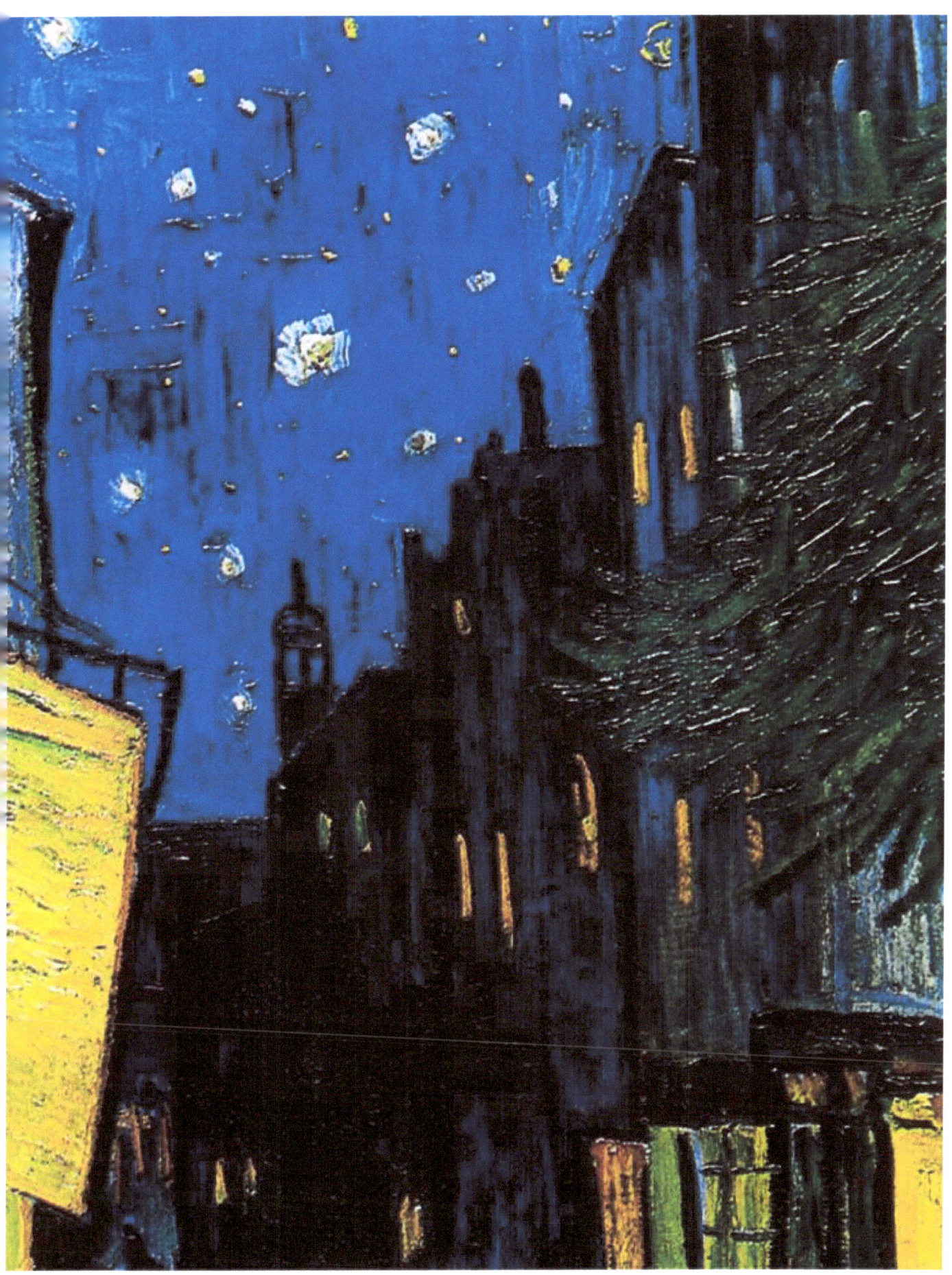

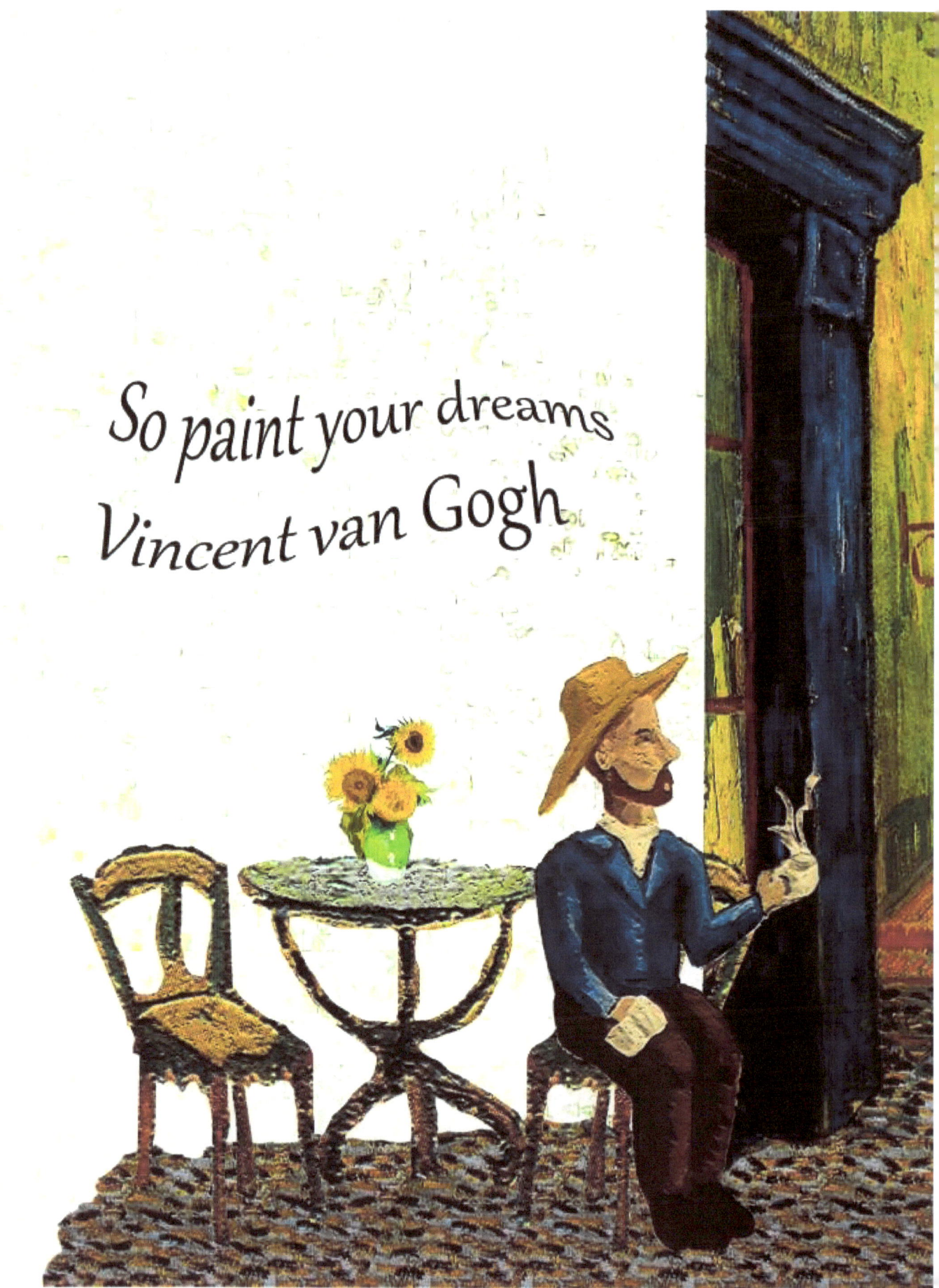

So paint your dreams Vincent van Gogh

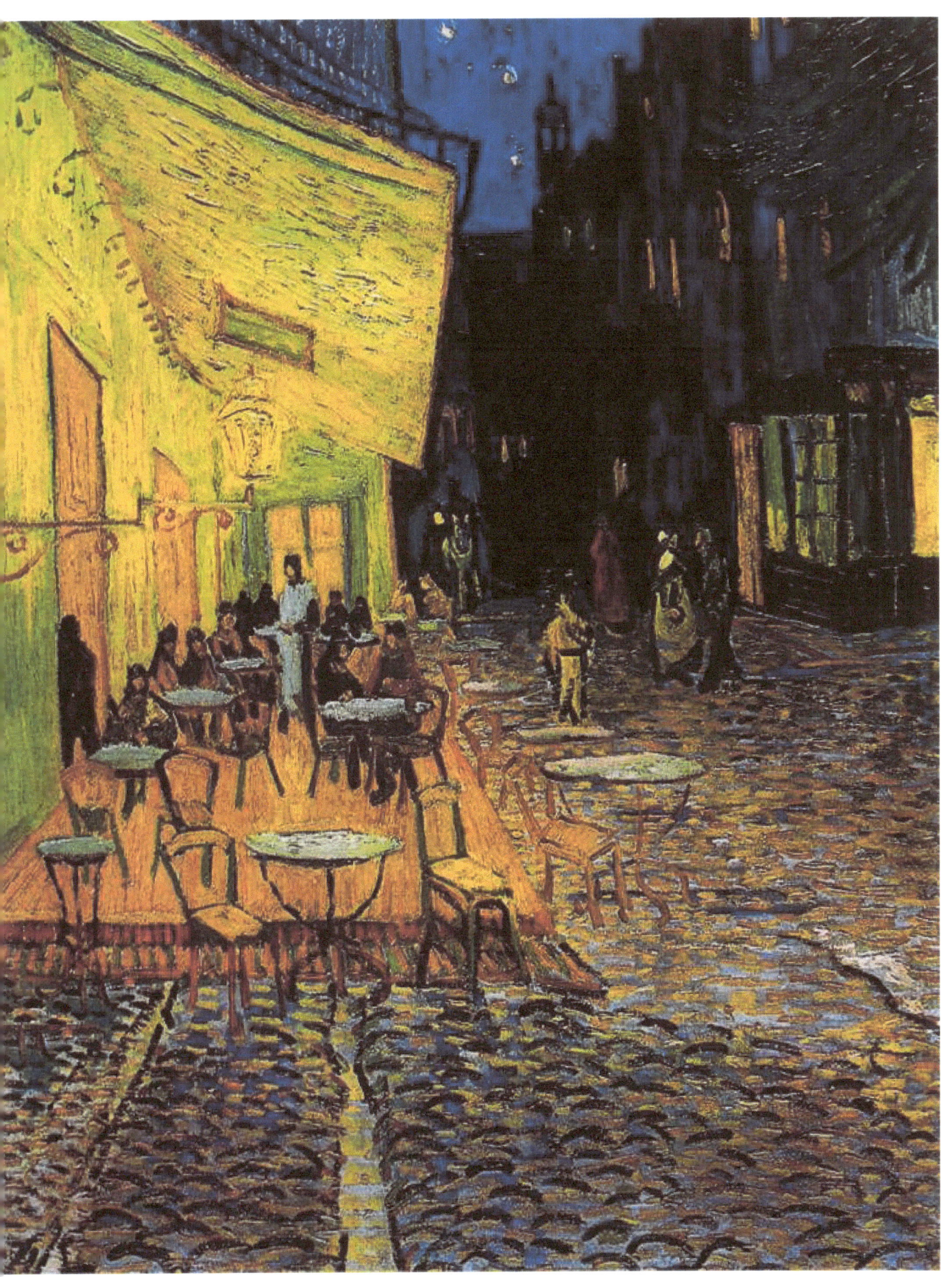

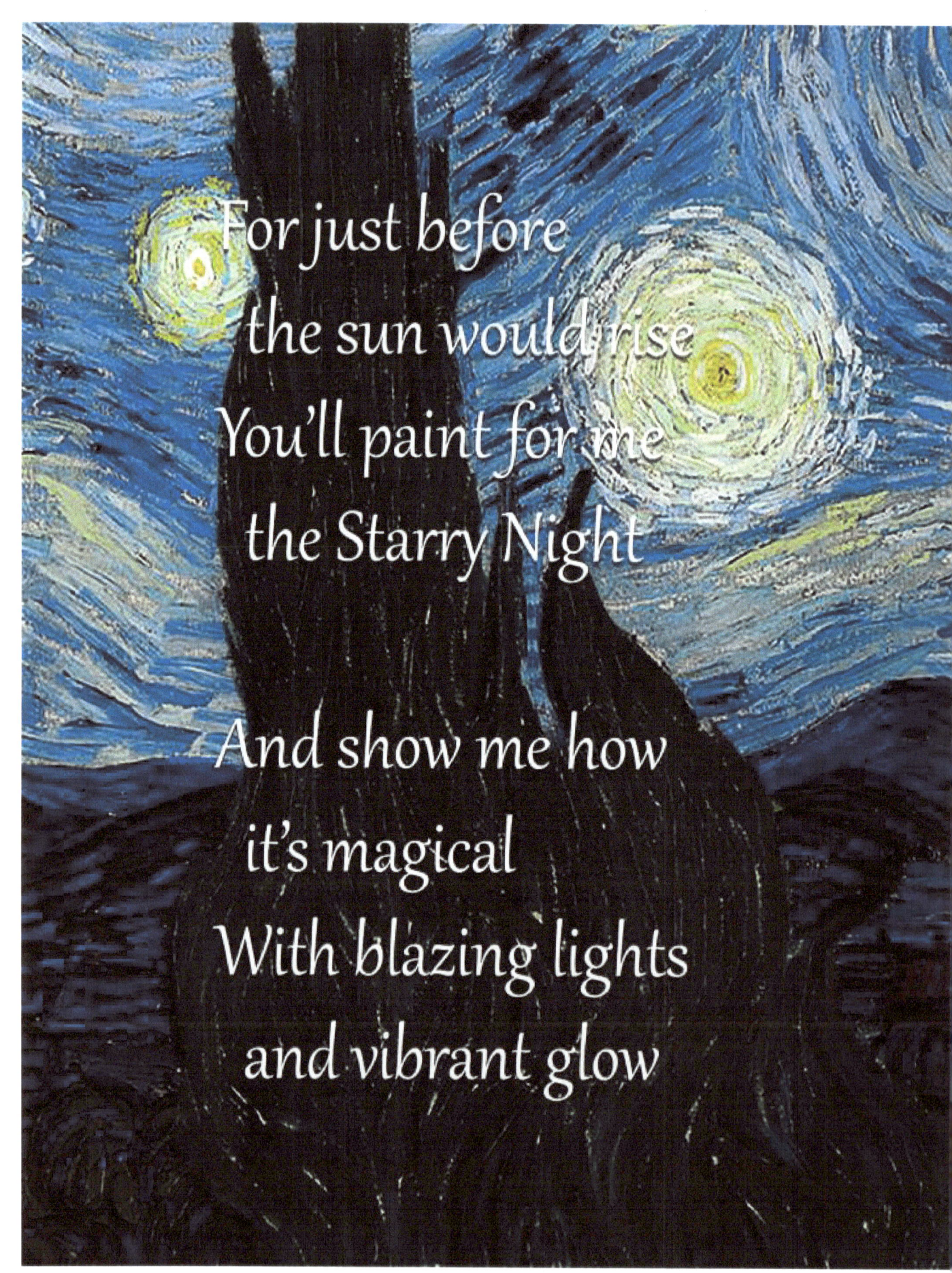

For just before
the sun would rise
You'll paint for me
the Starry Night

And show me how
it's magical
With blazing lights
and vibrant glow

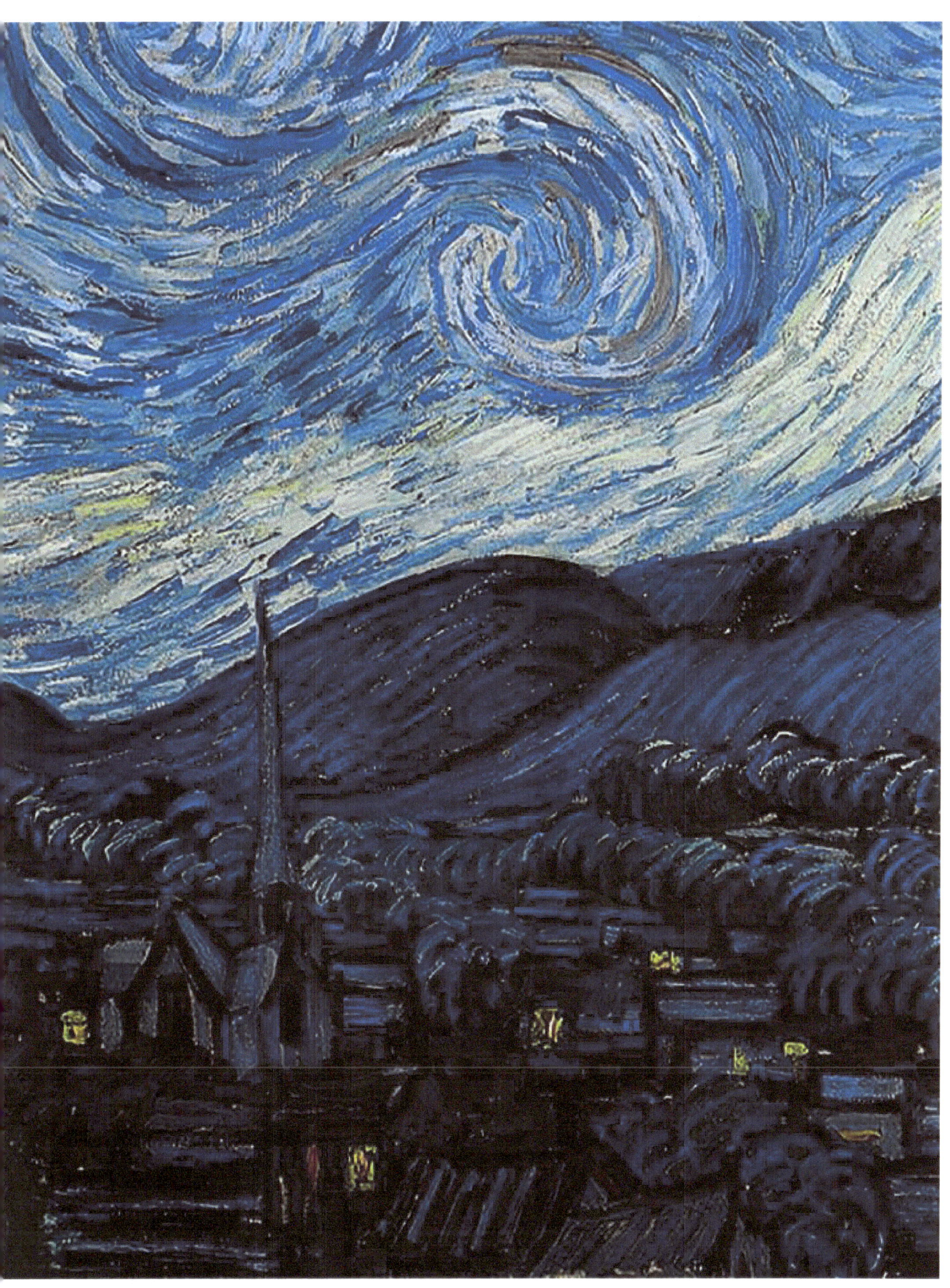

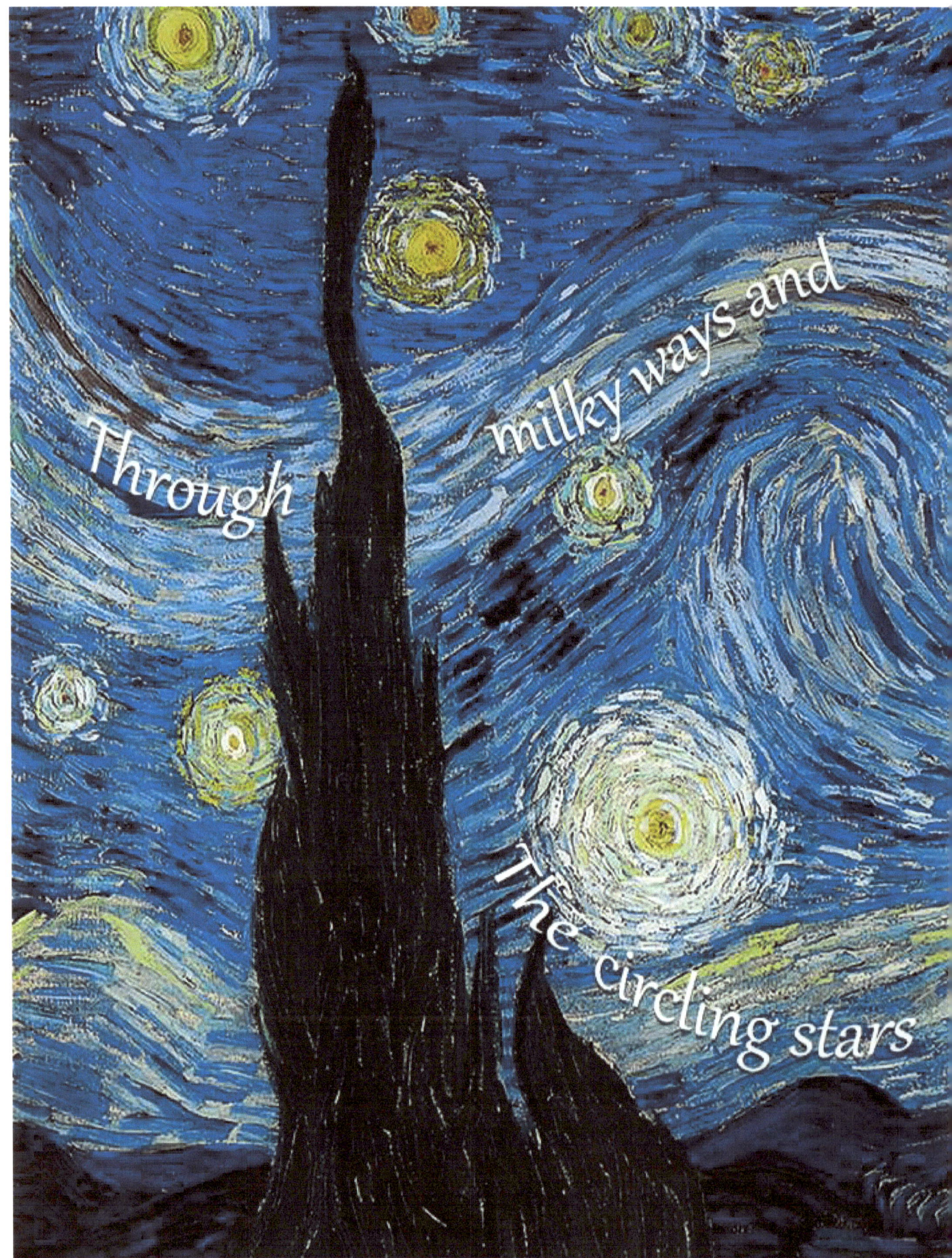

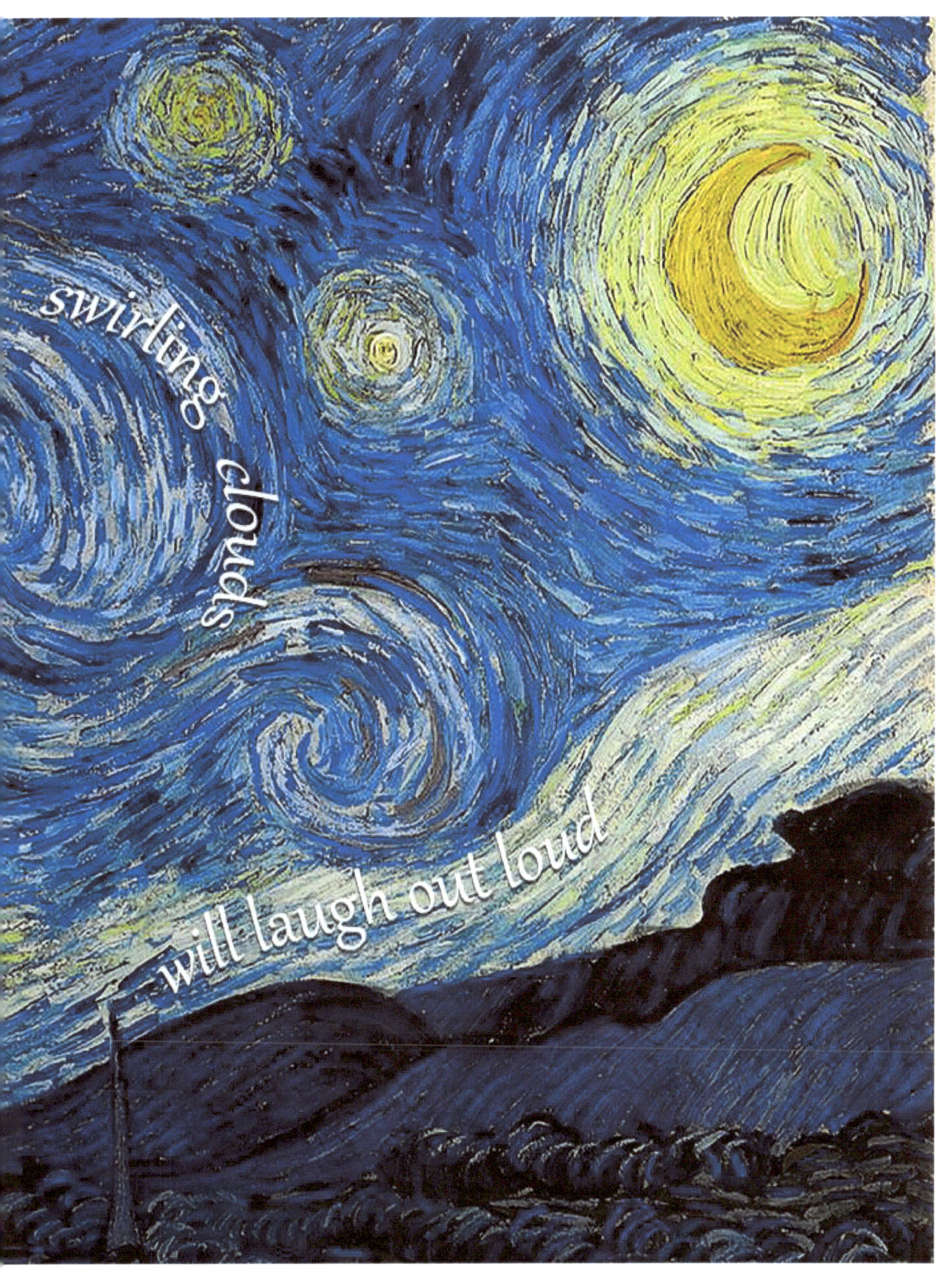

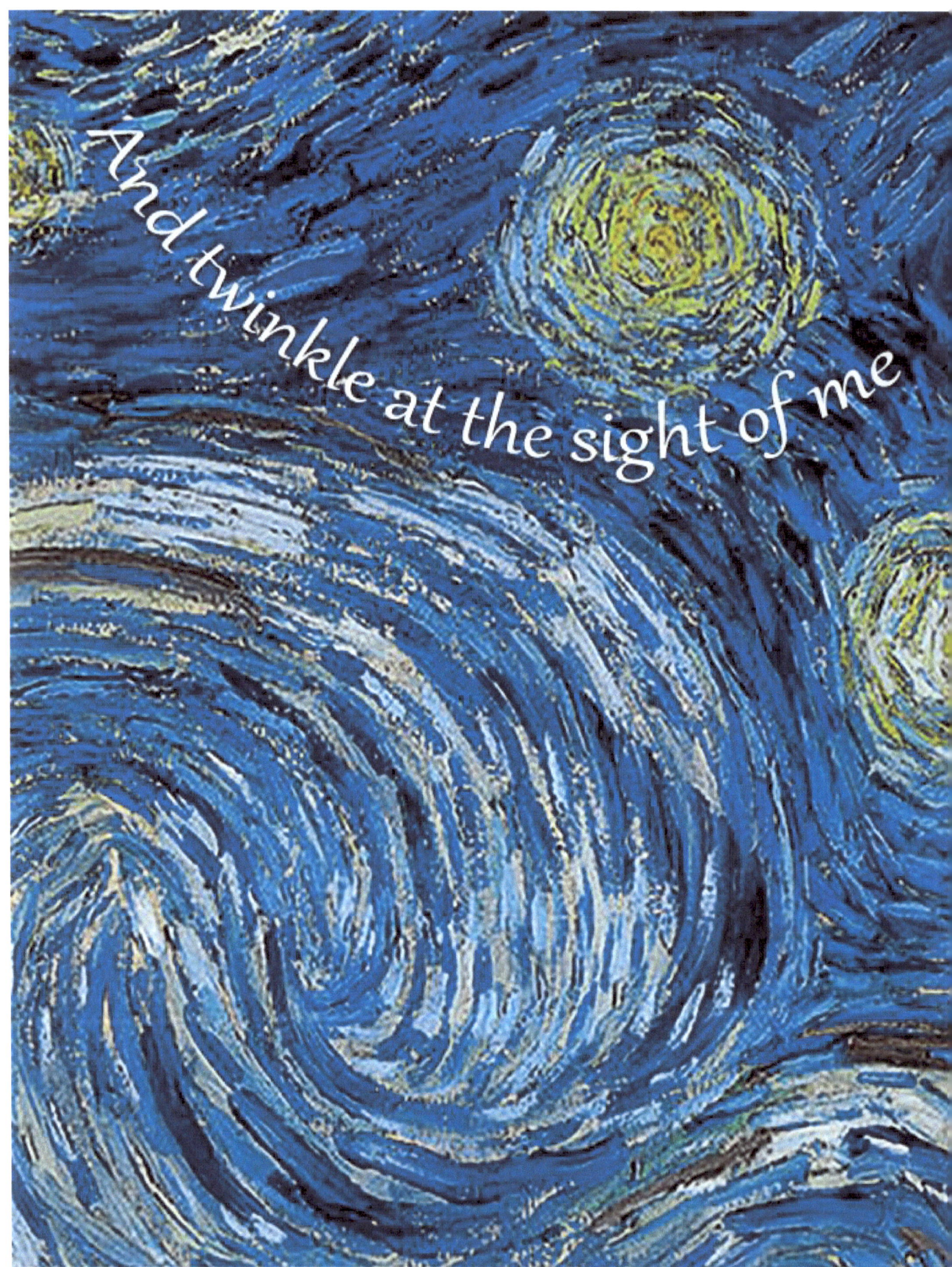

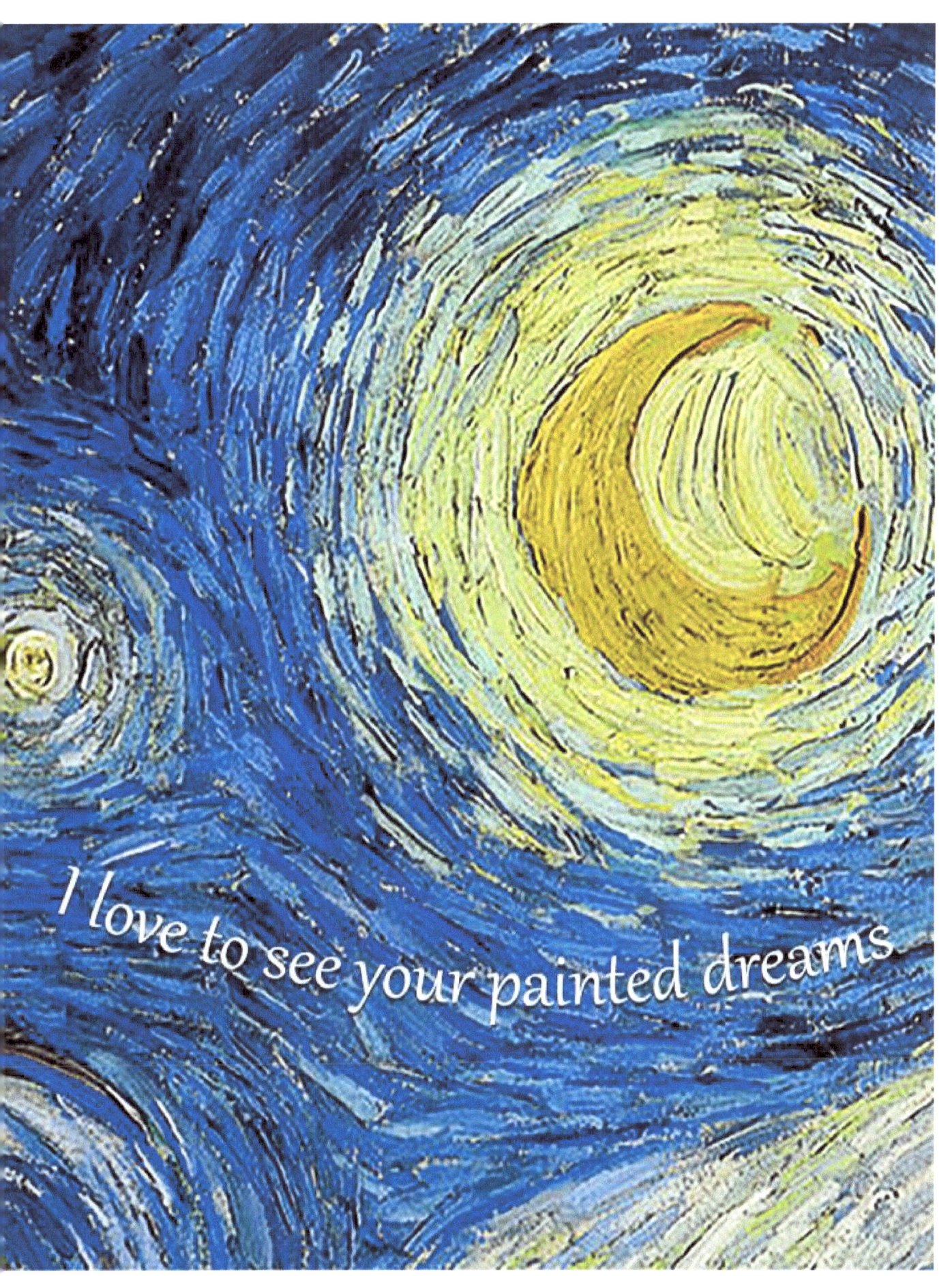

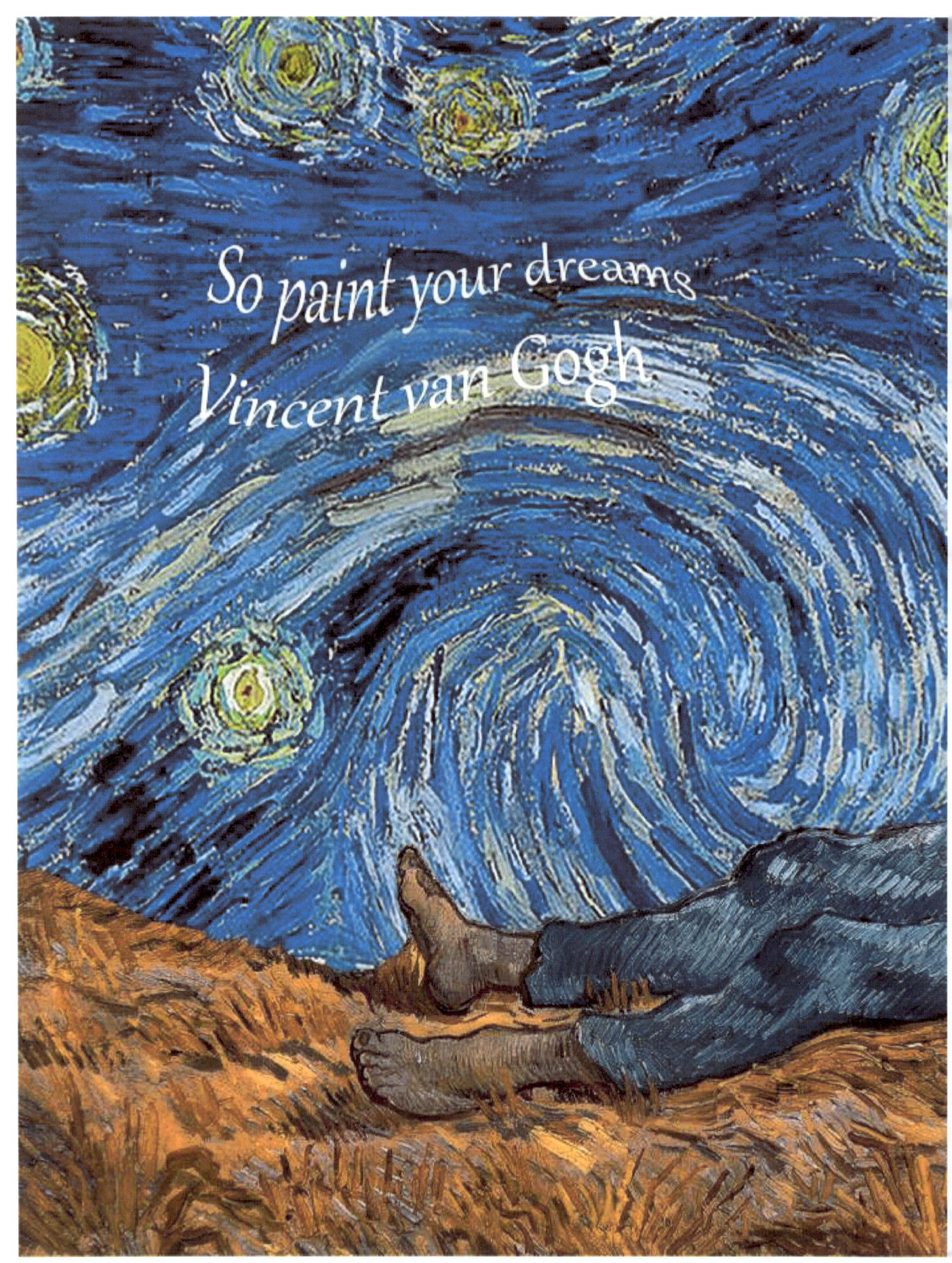

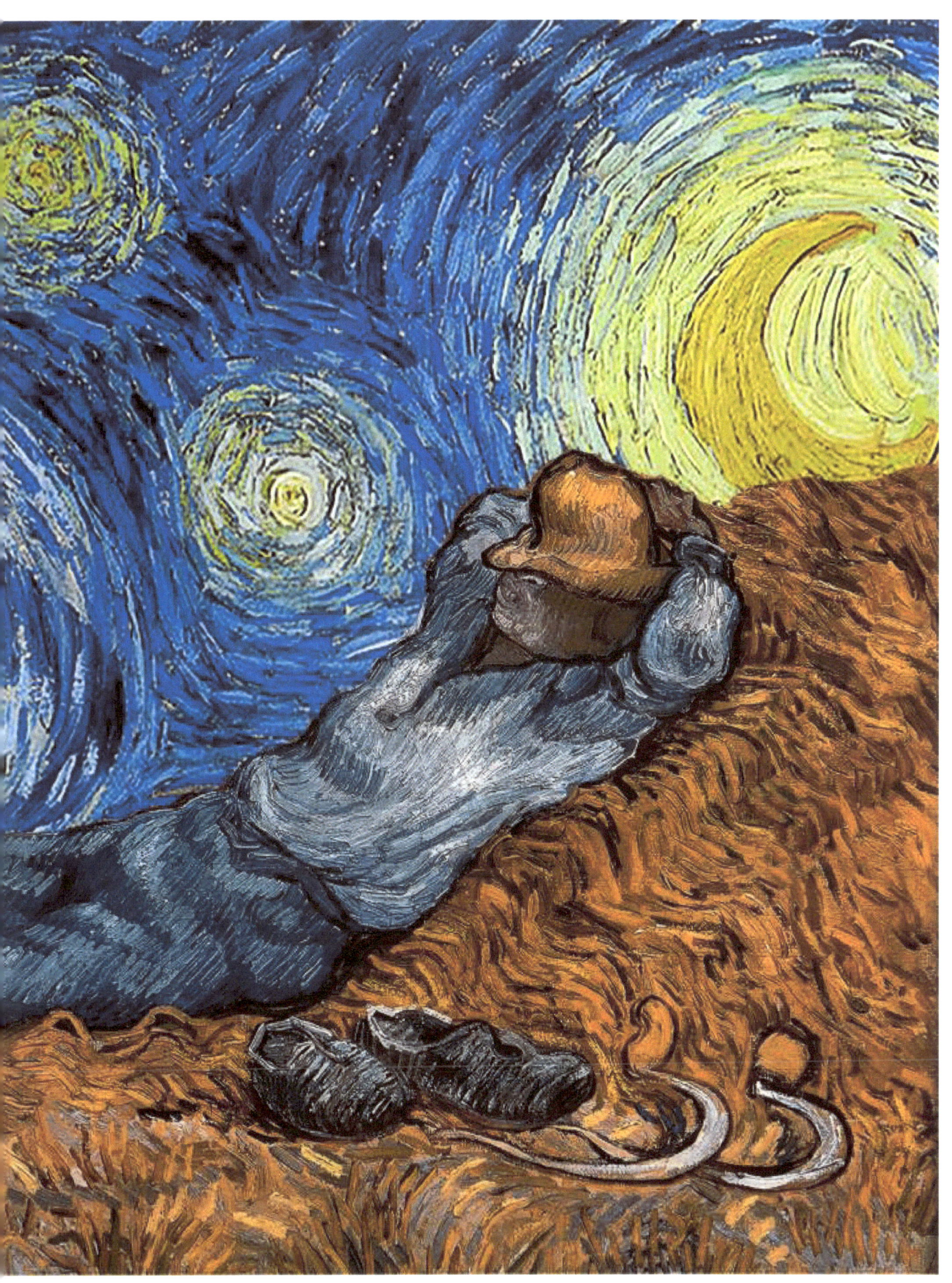

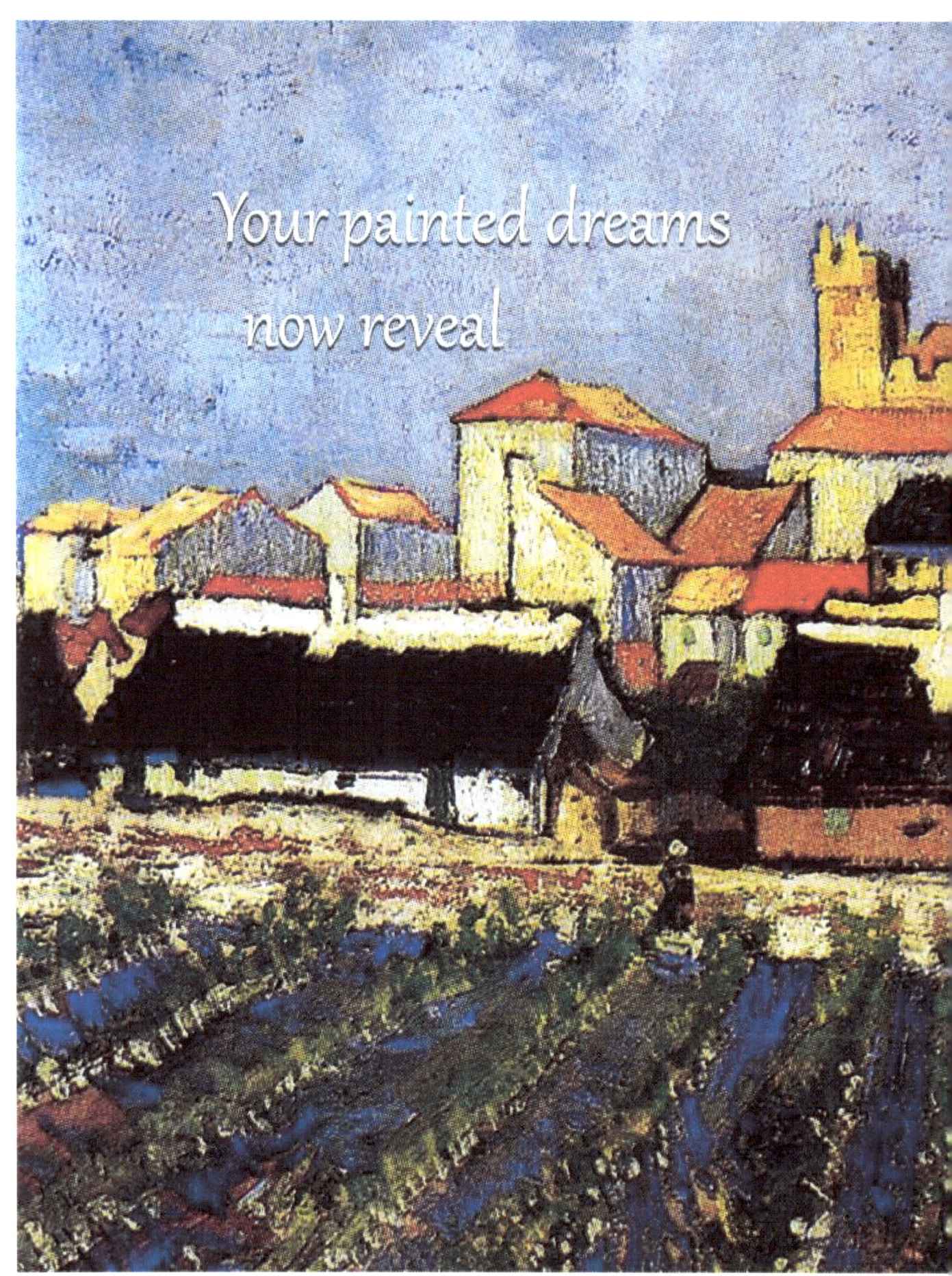

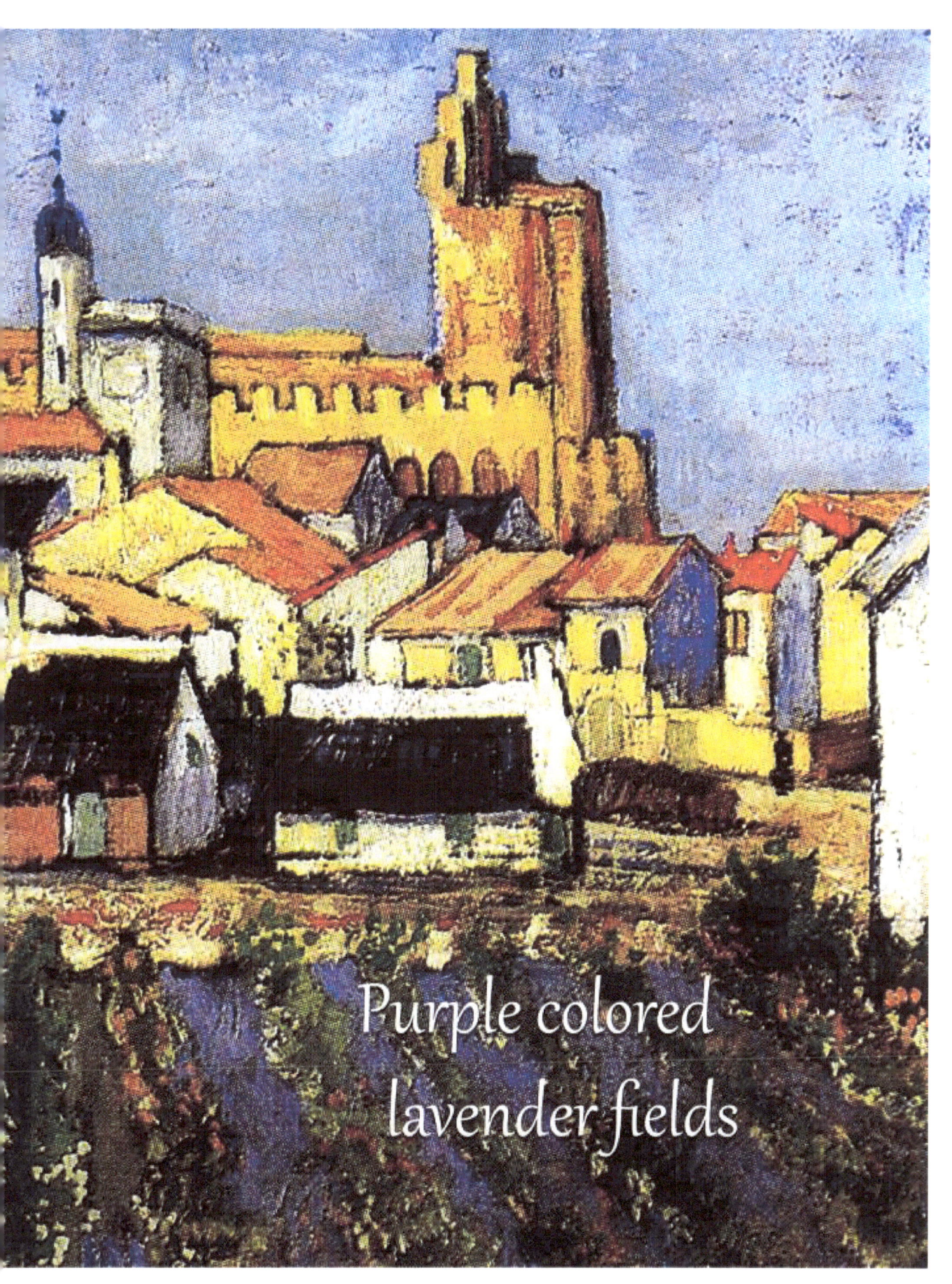

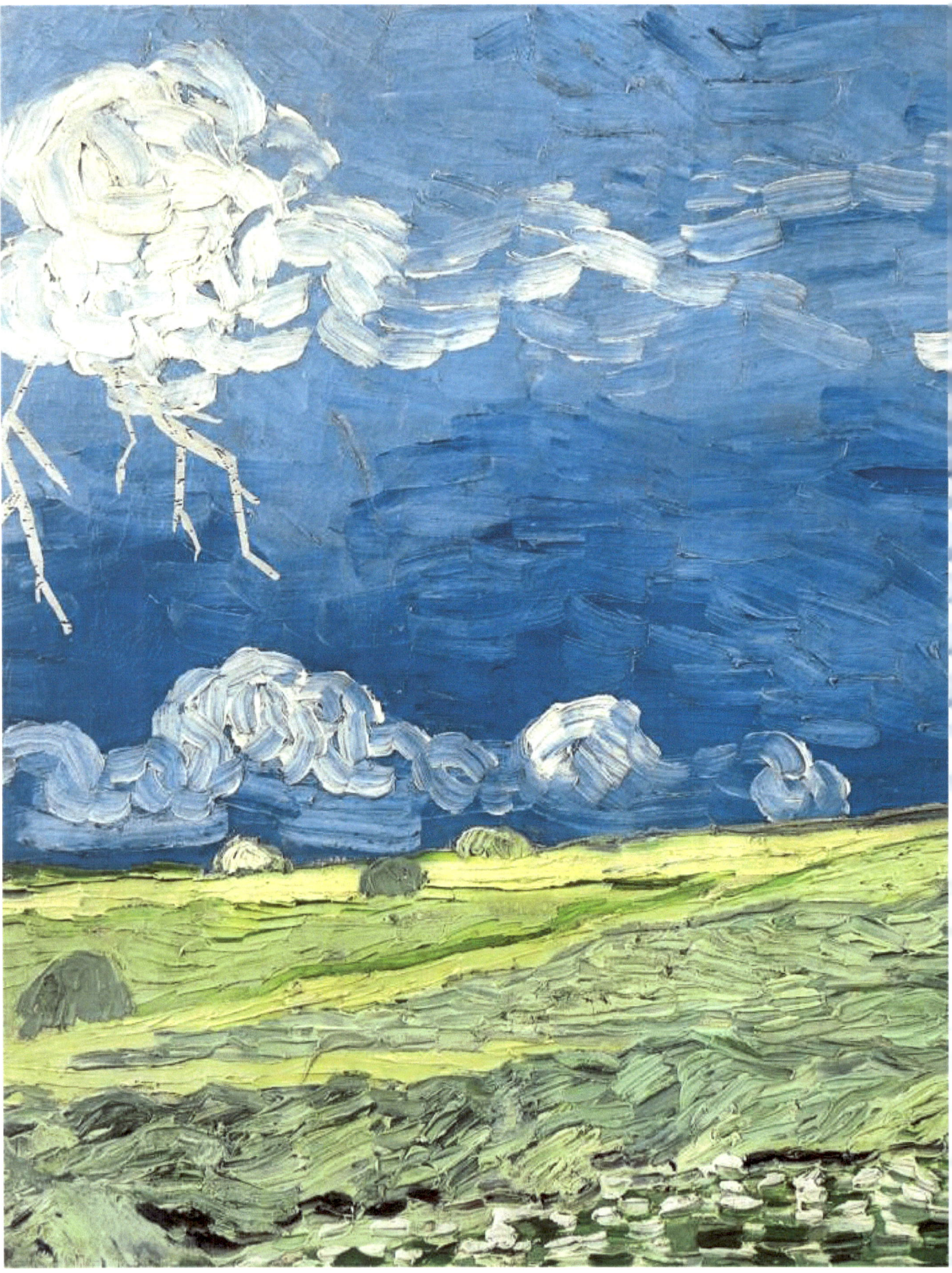

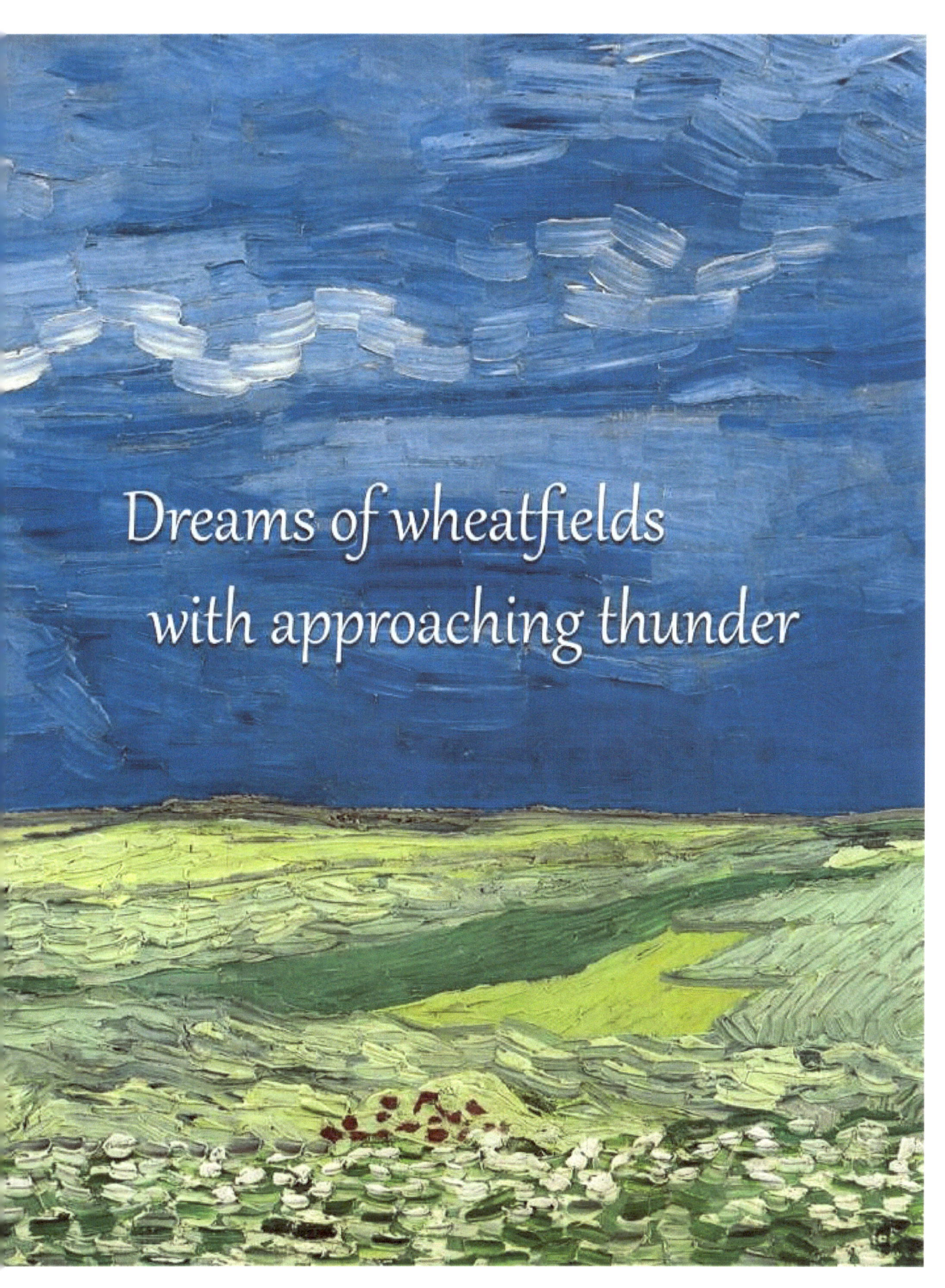

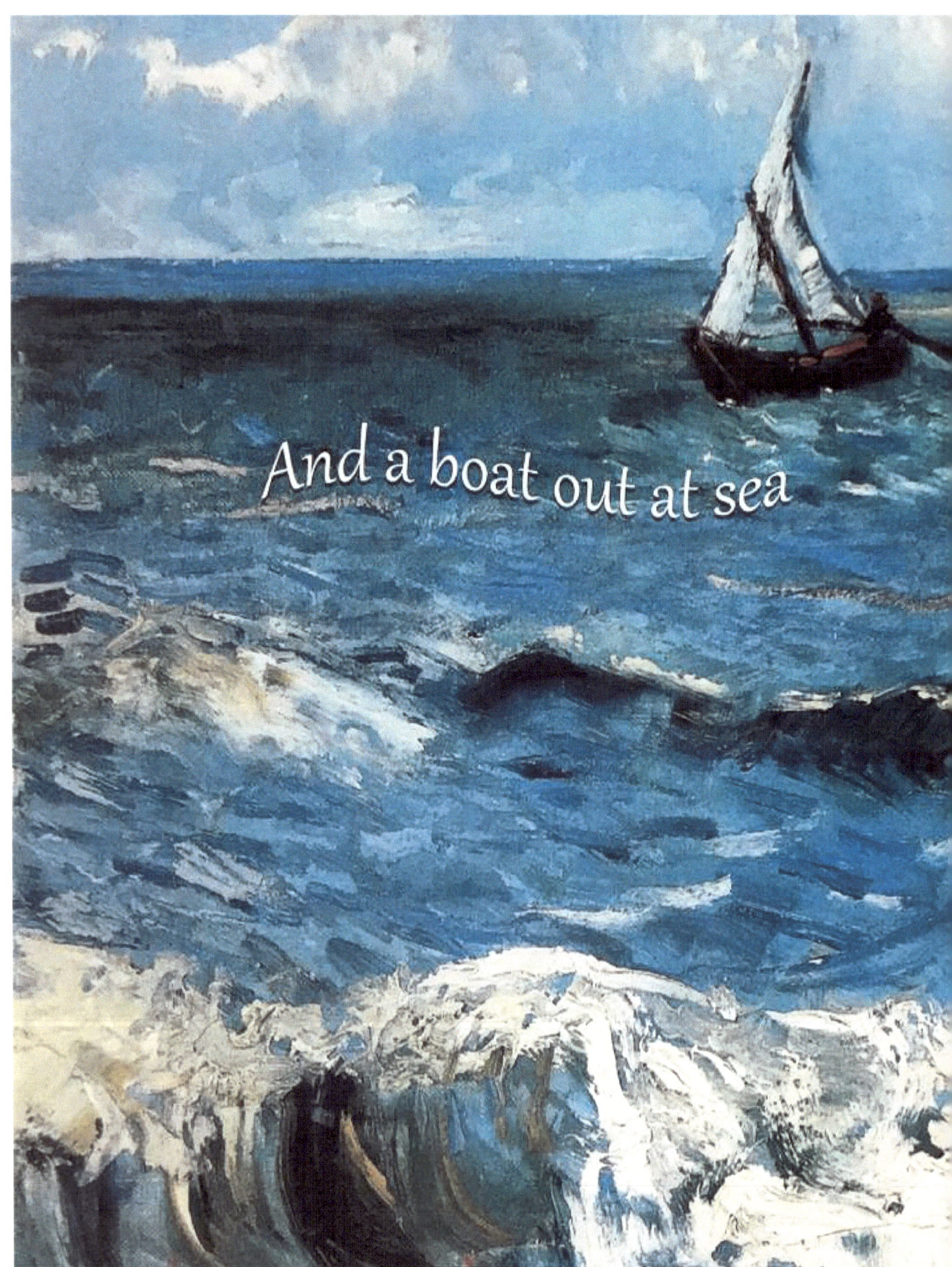

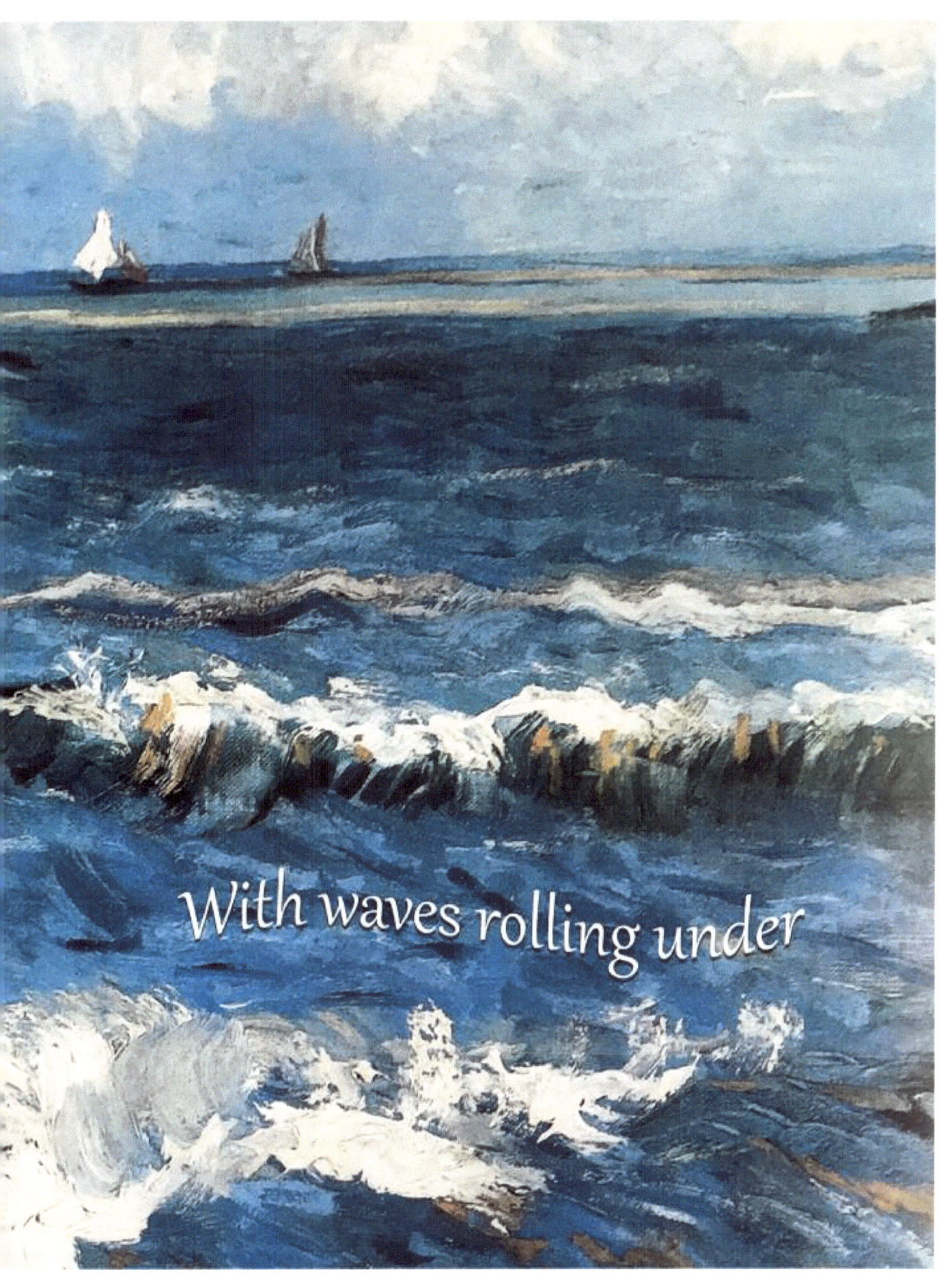

So paint your dreams
Vincent van Gogh

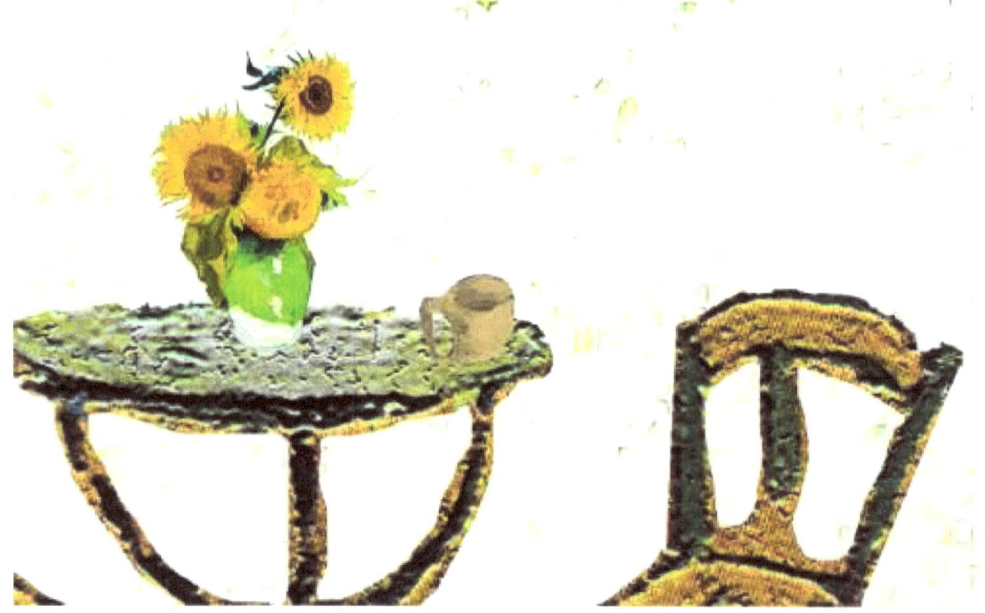
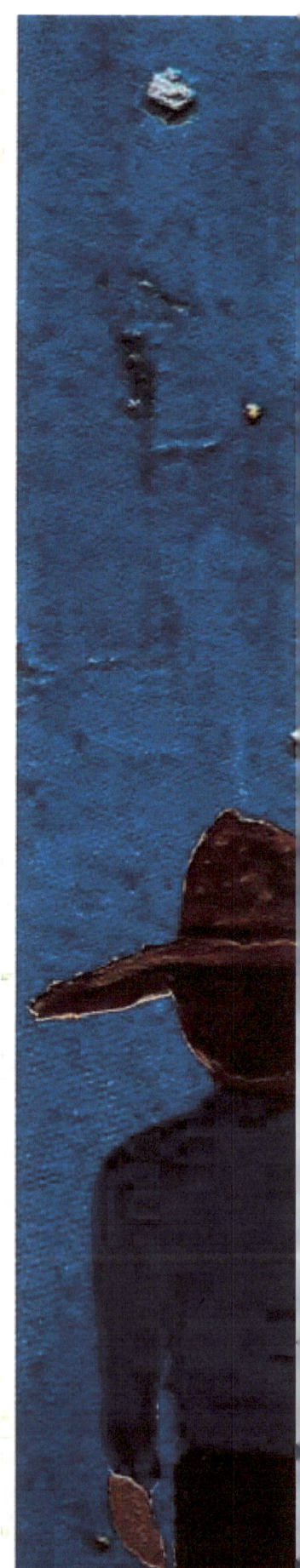

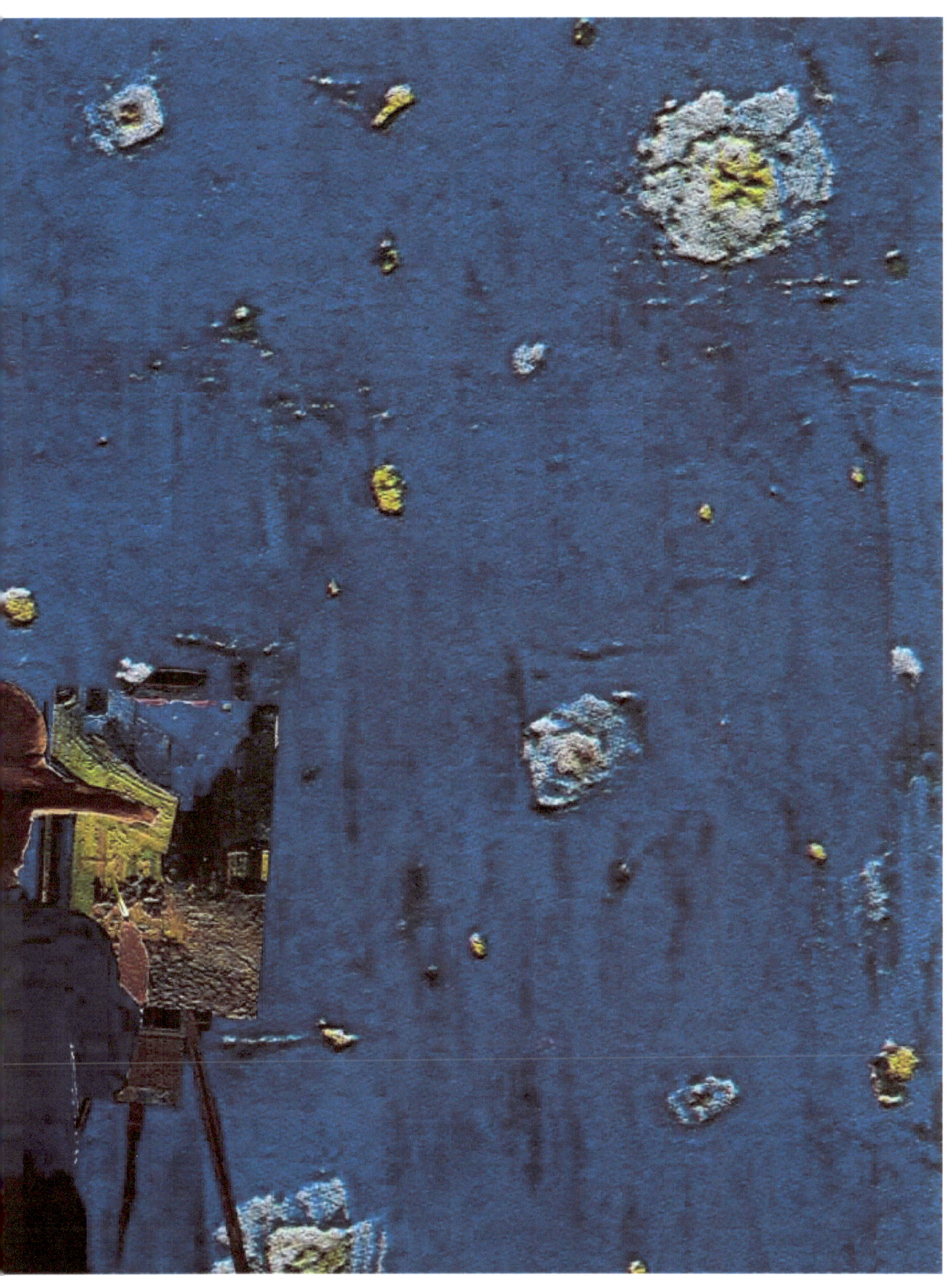

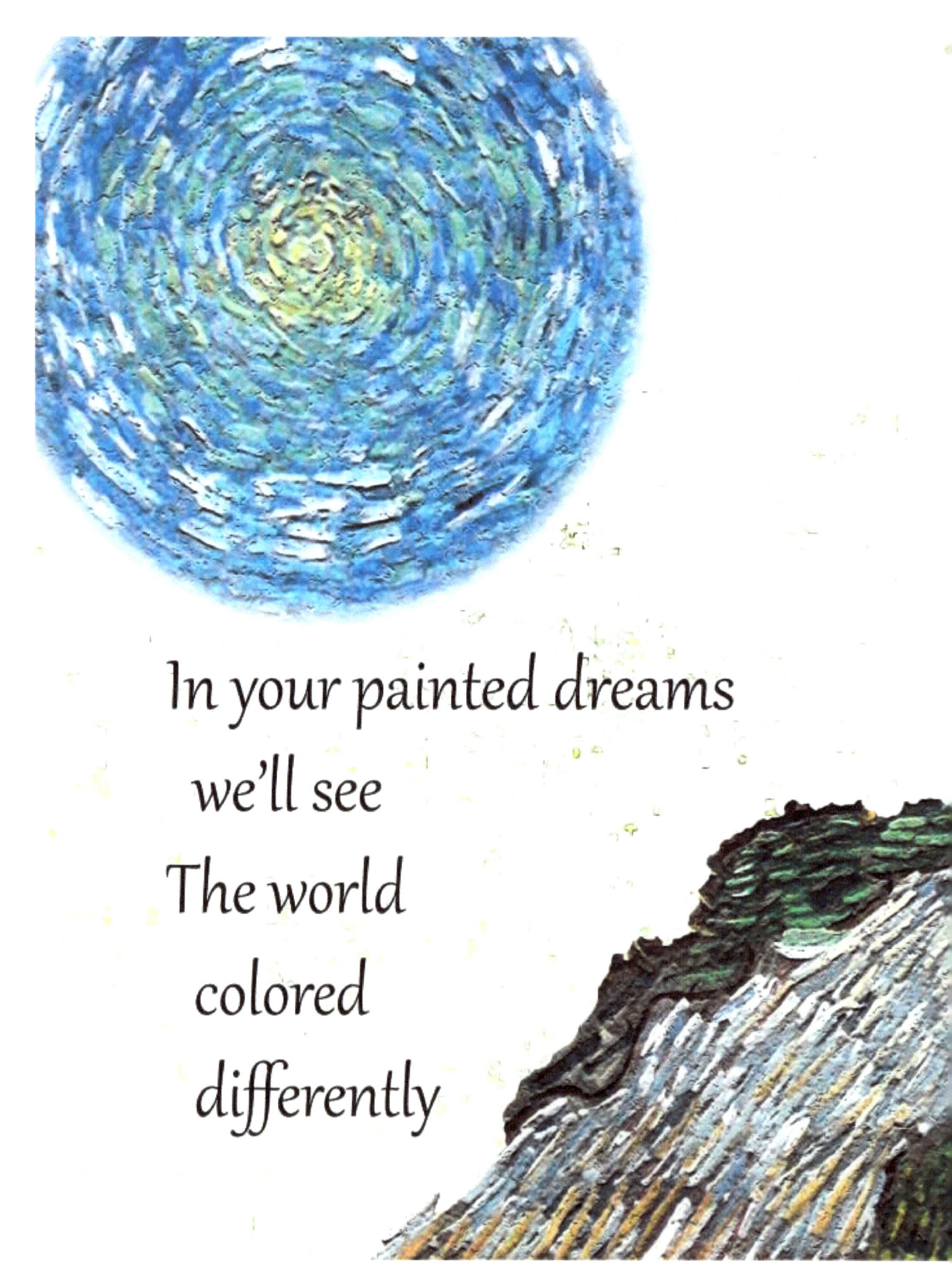

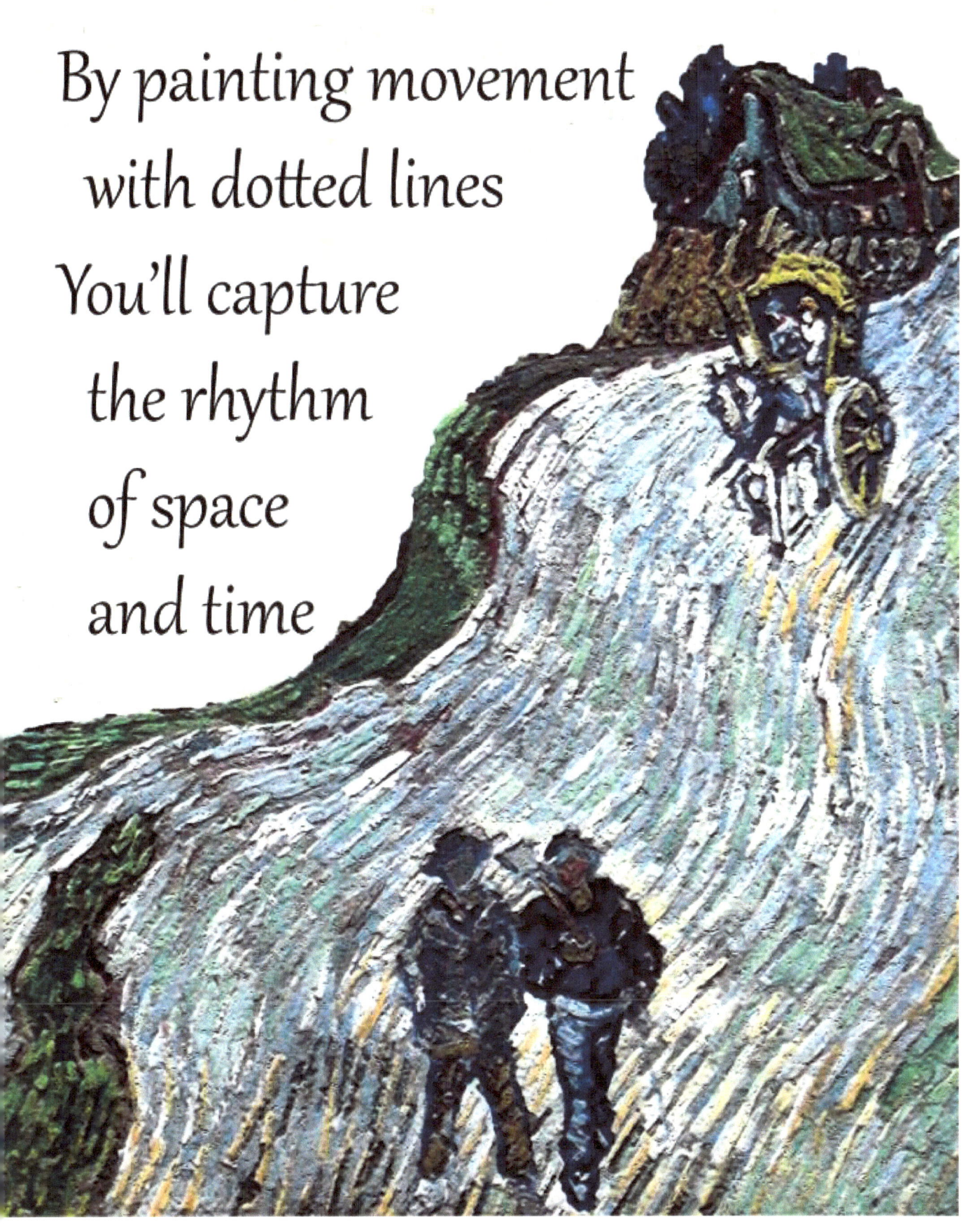

By painting movement
with dotted lines
You'll capture
the rhythm
of space
and time

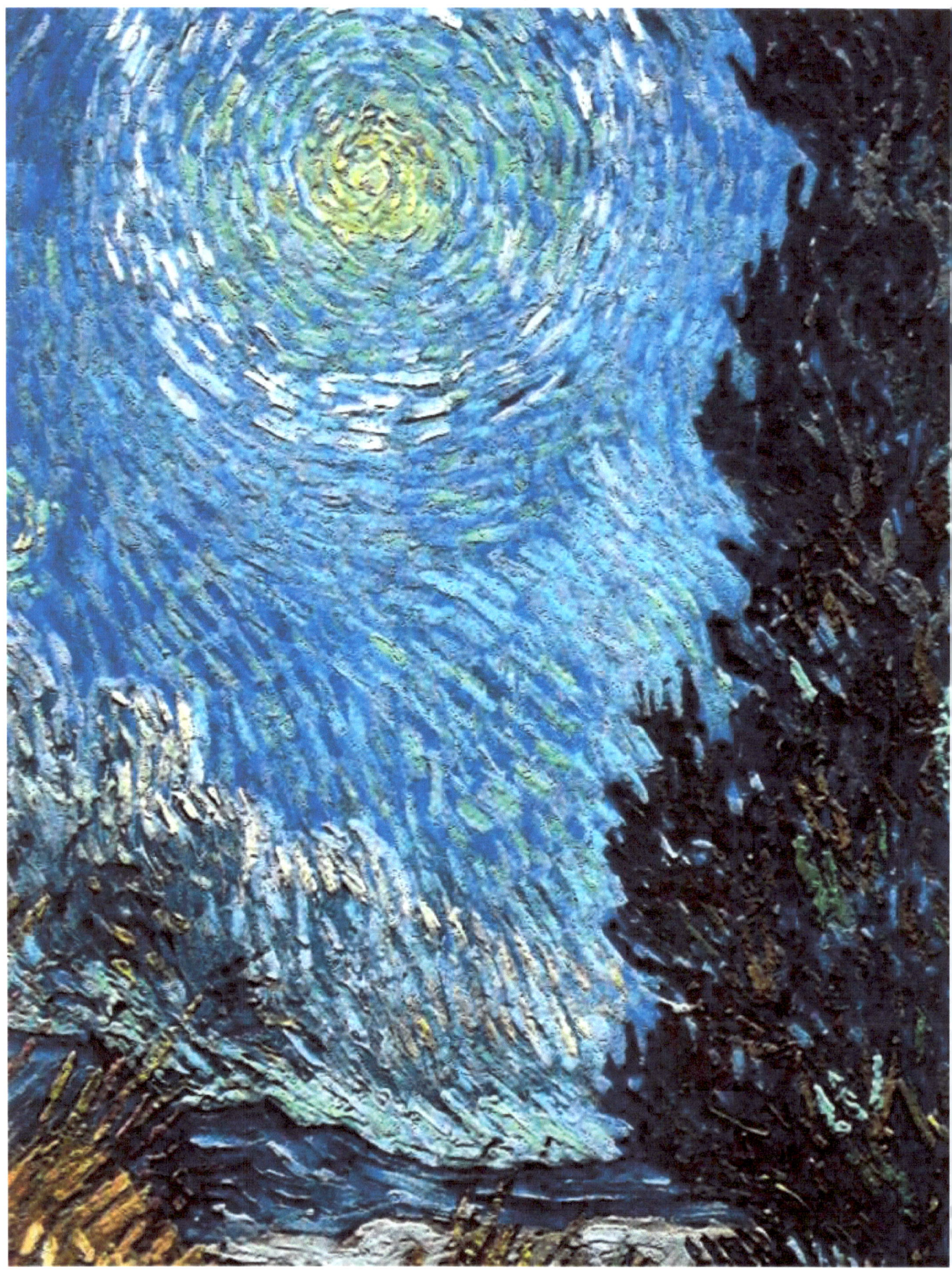

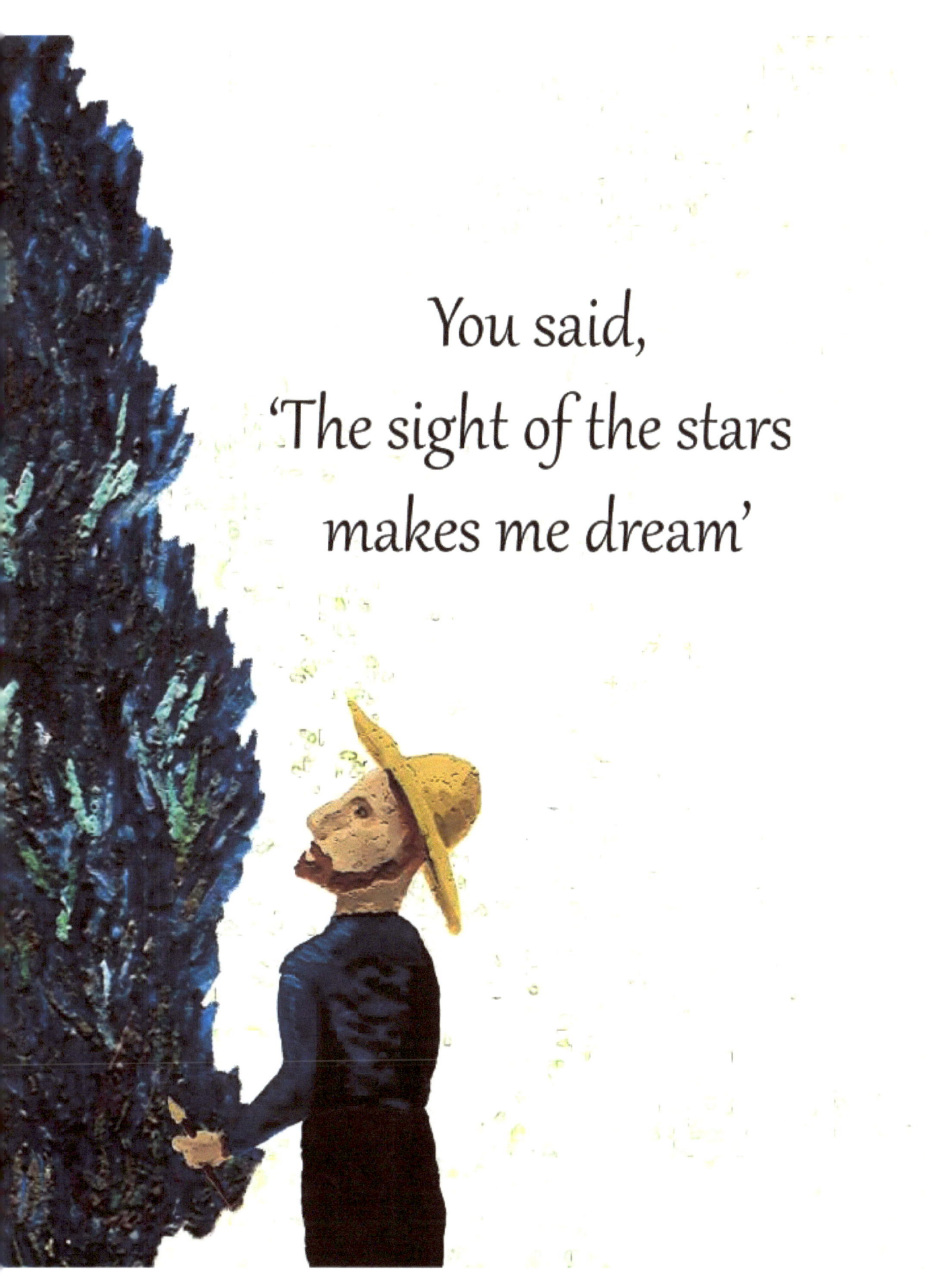

So you climbed up high
in a cypress tree

Dreaming the dreams
of stars and soon

You climbed so high
you touched the moon

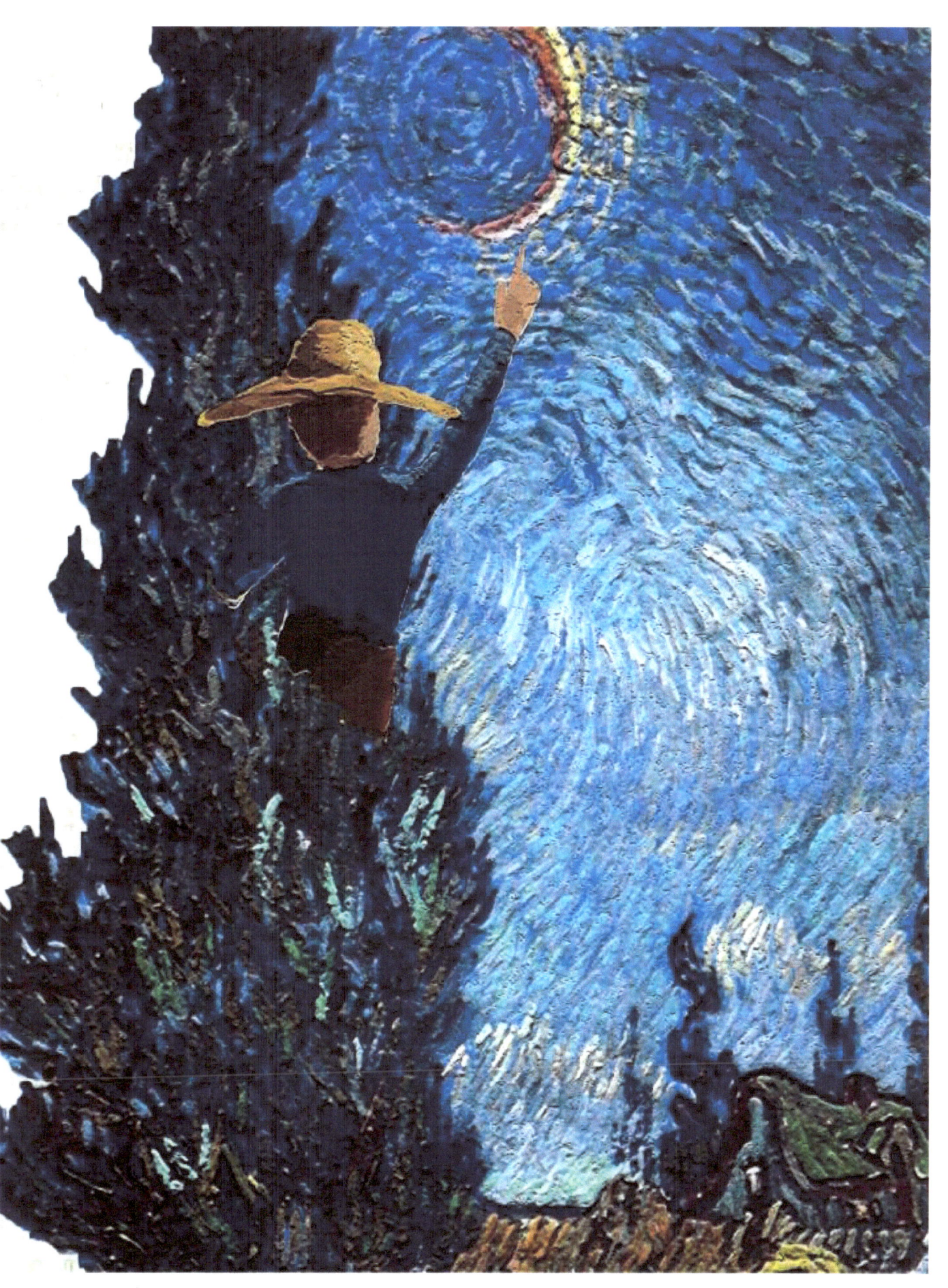

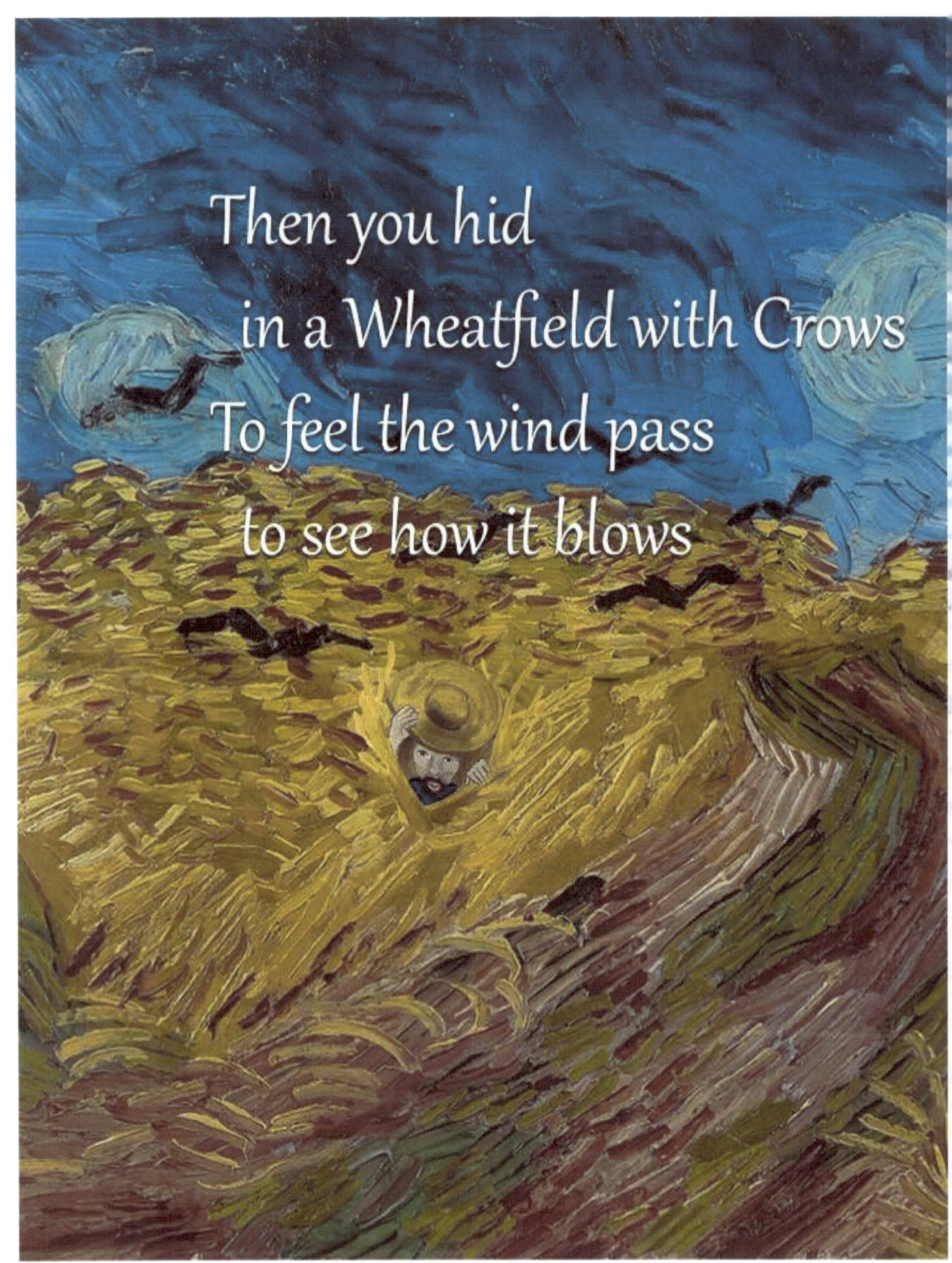

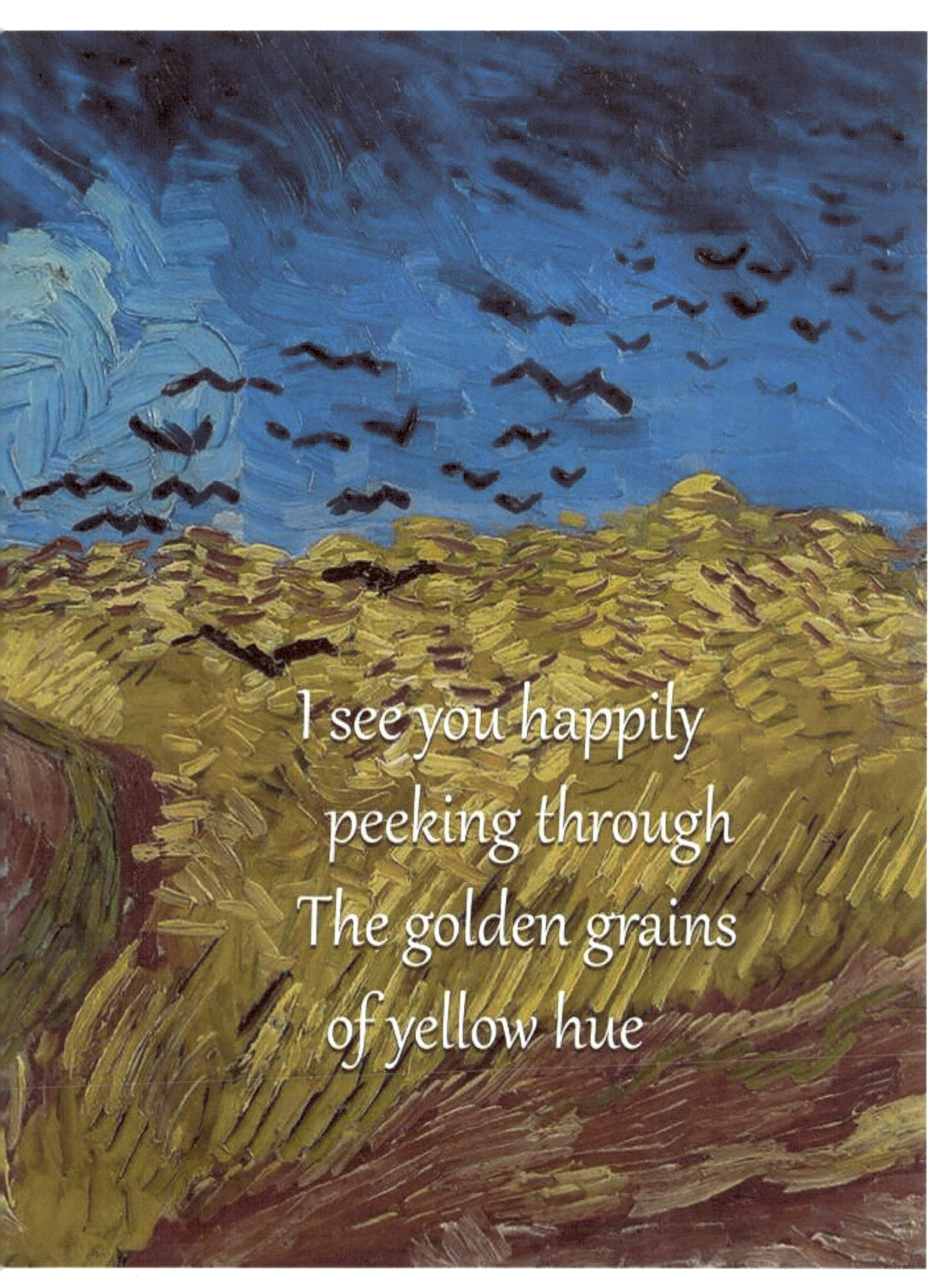

Then found you sitting patiently

Underneath

Falling Autumn Leaves

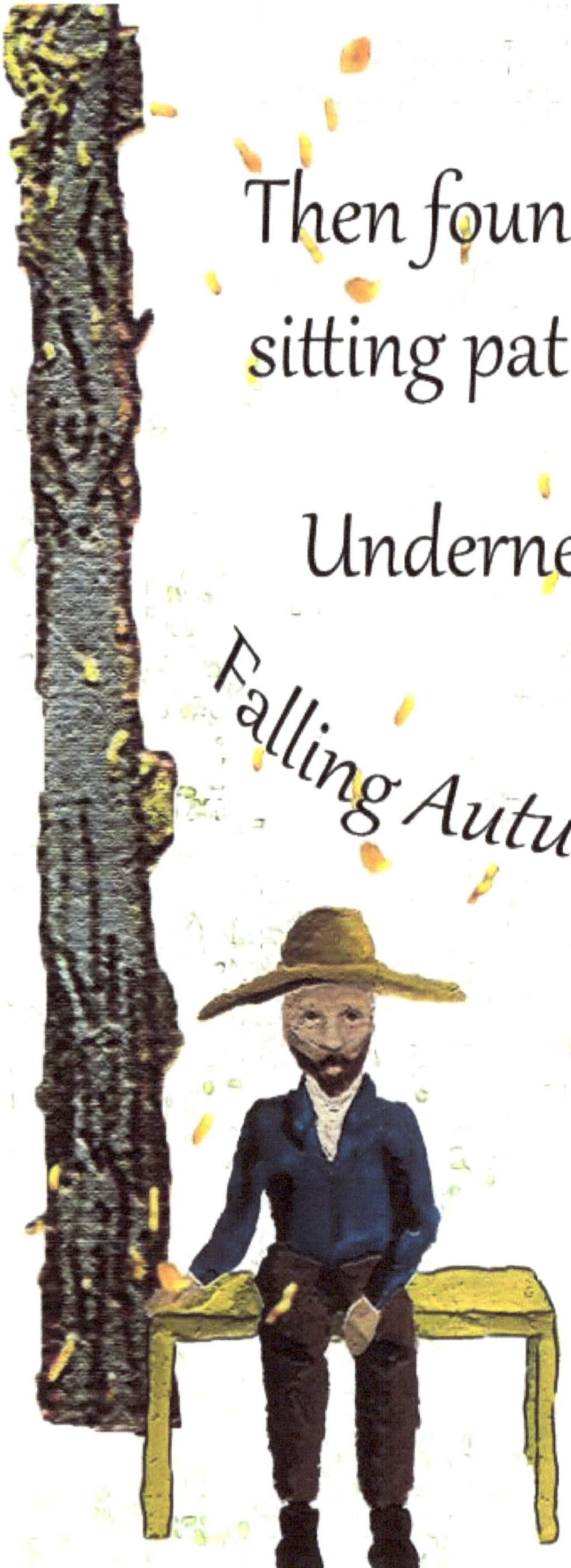

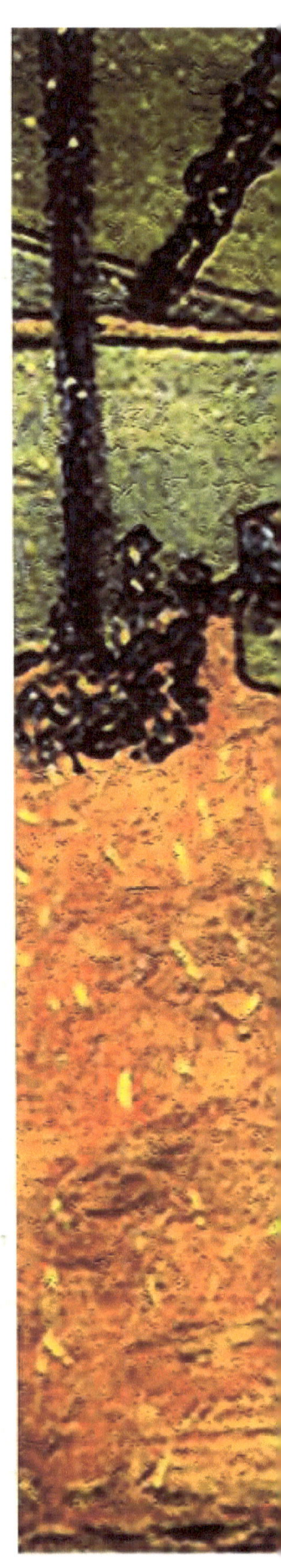

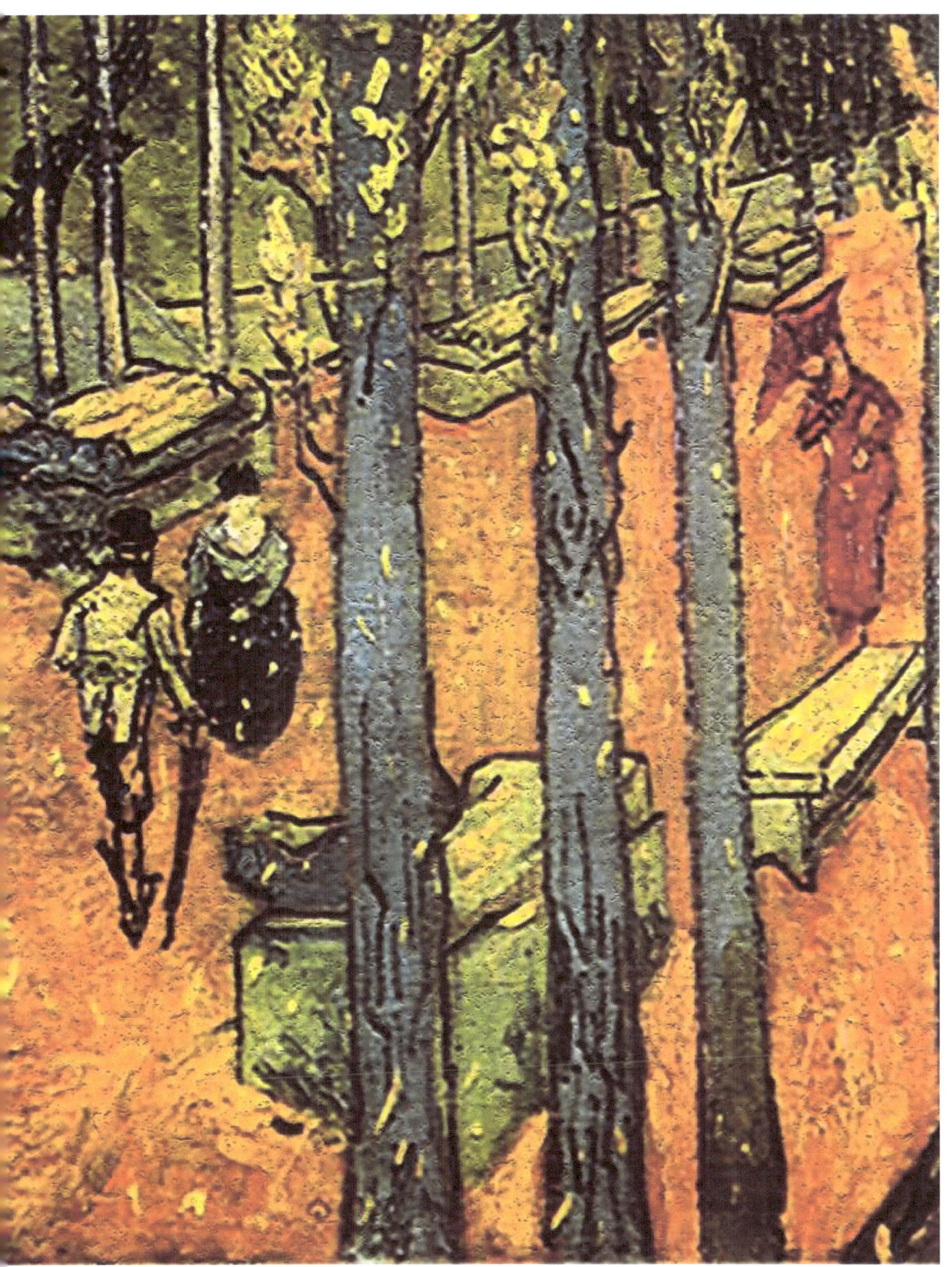

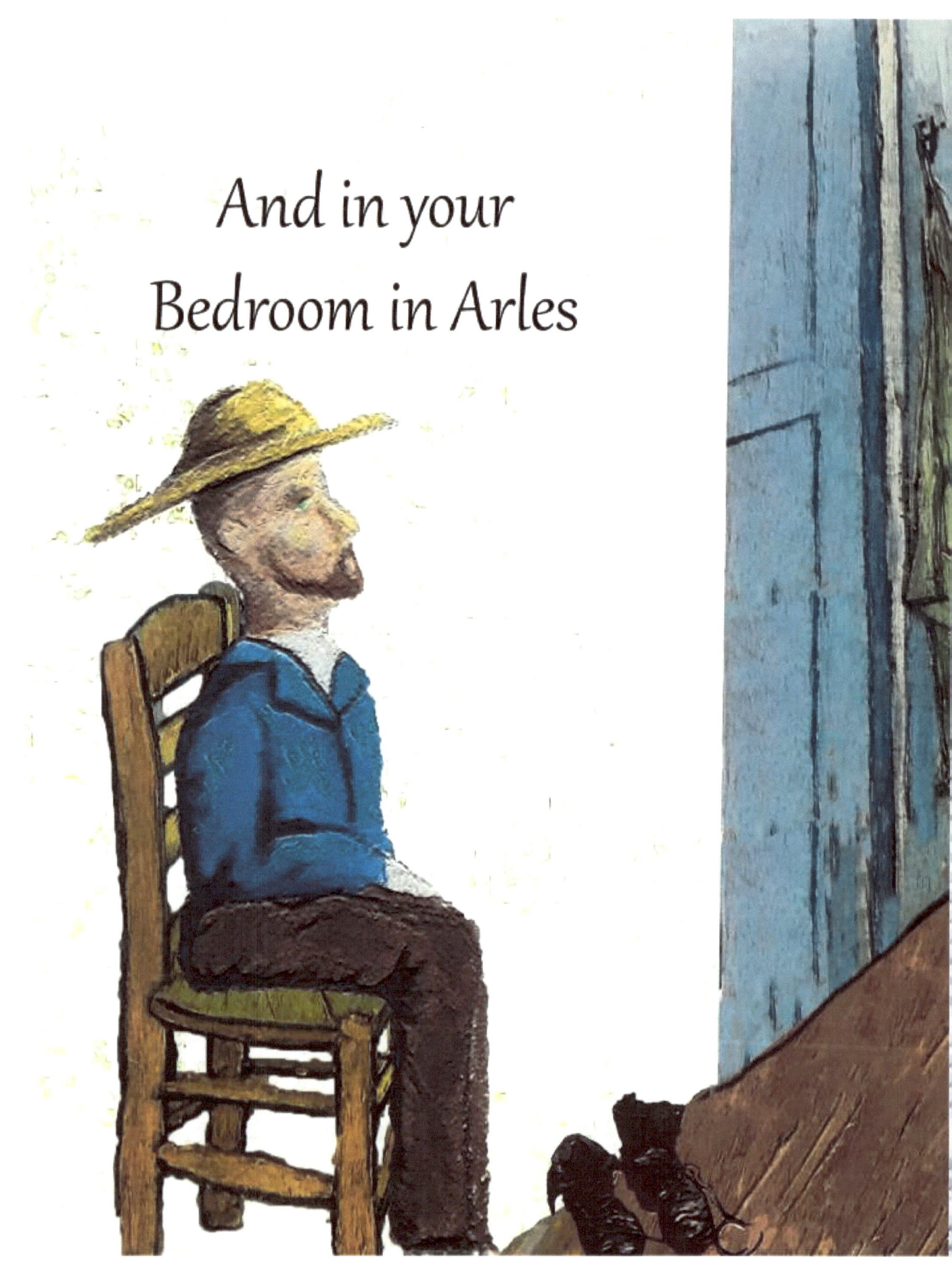

And in your Bedroom in Arles

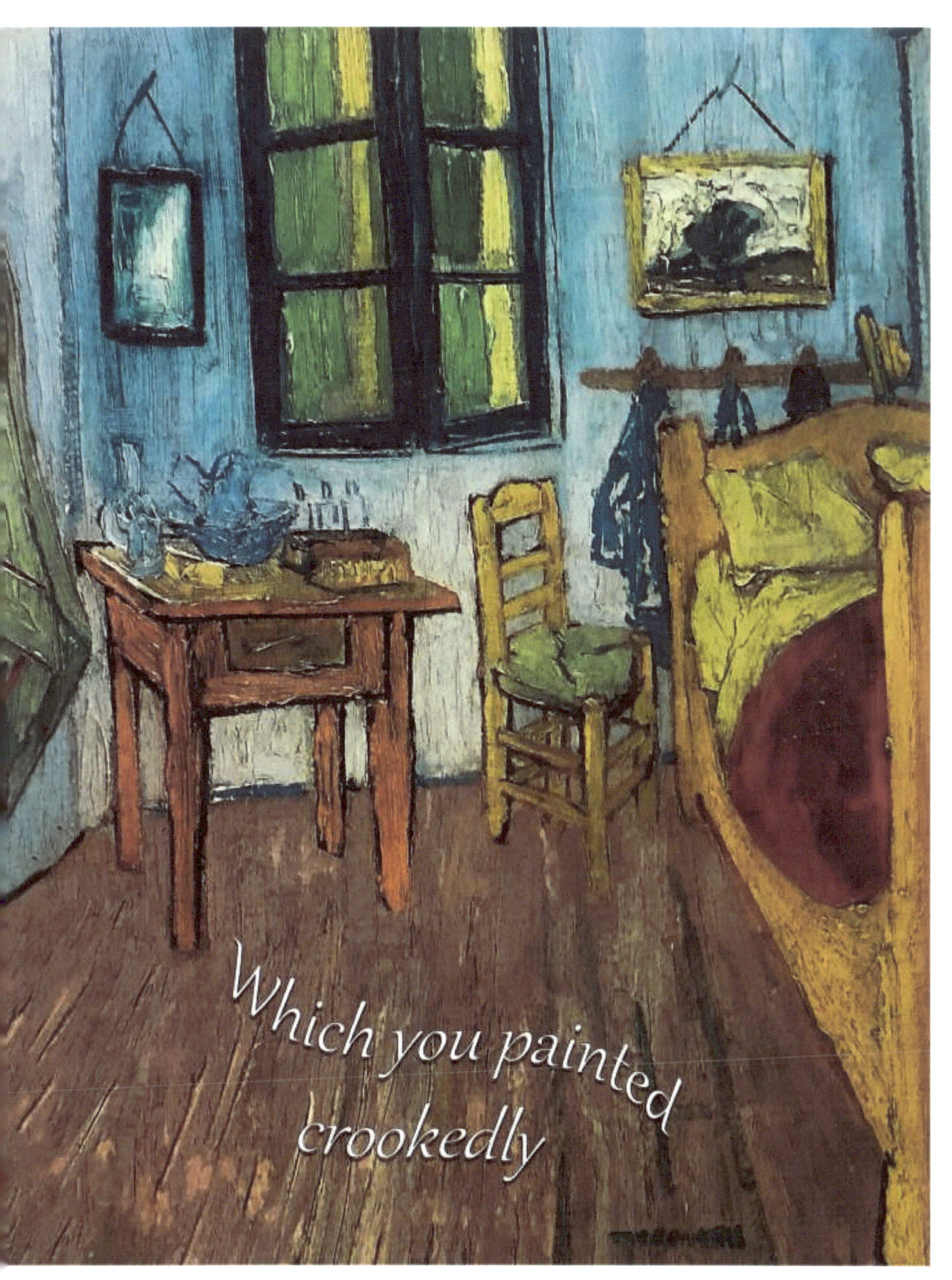

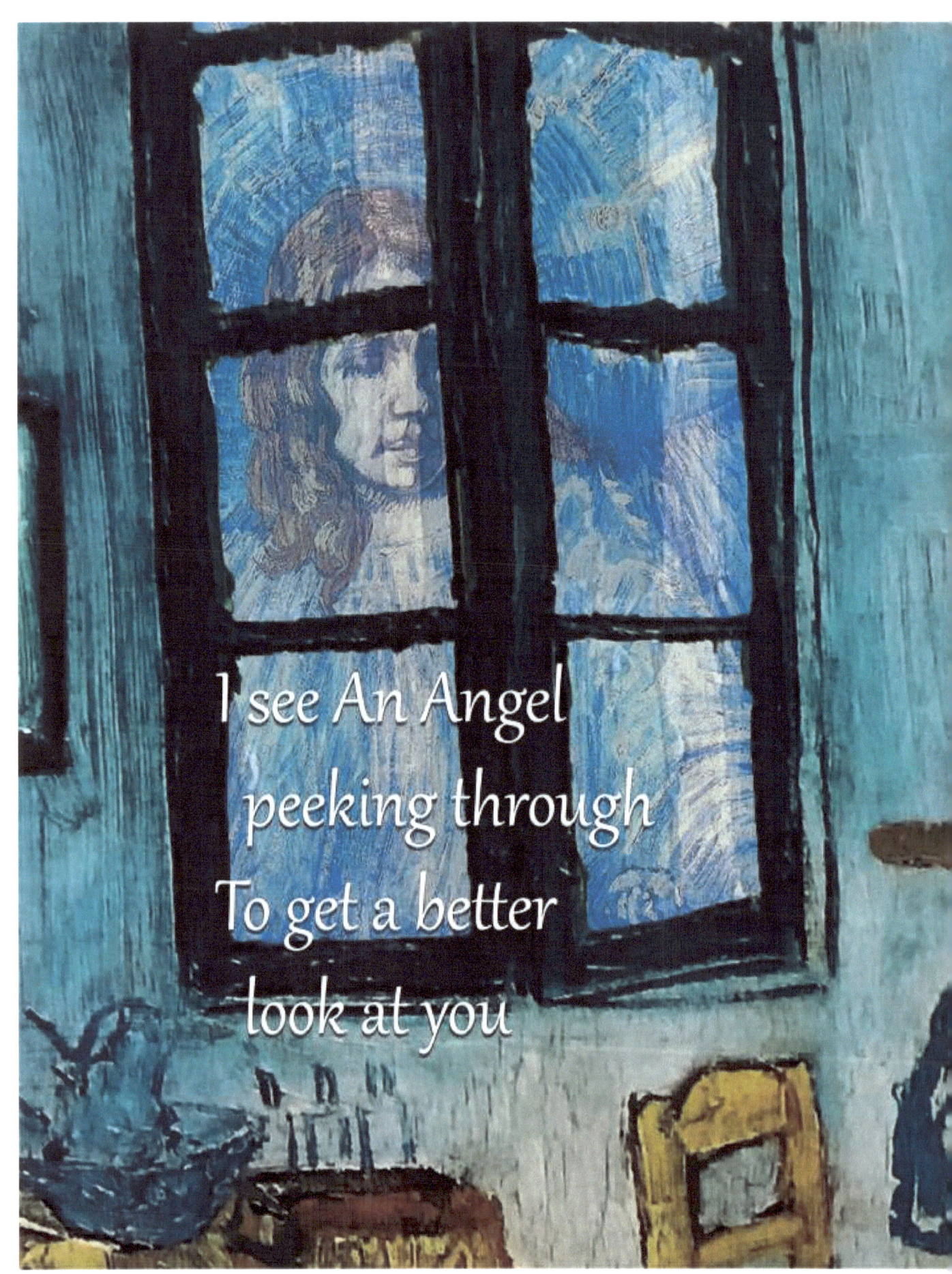

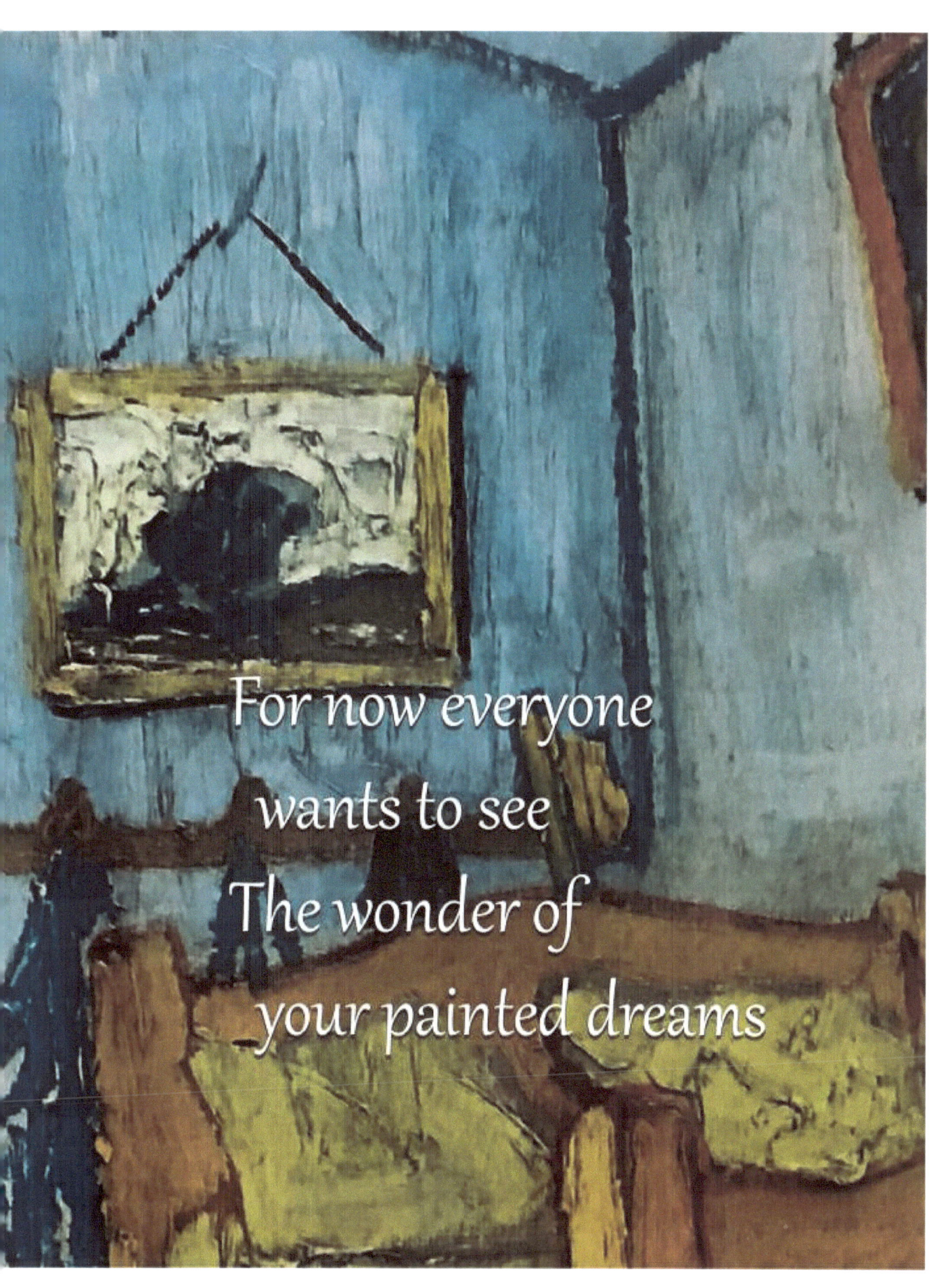

Like Vincent Van Gogh
You can paint
your dreams too

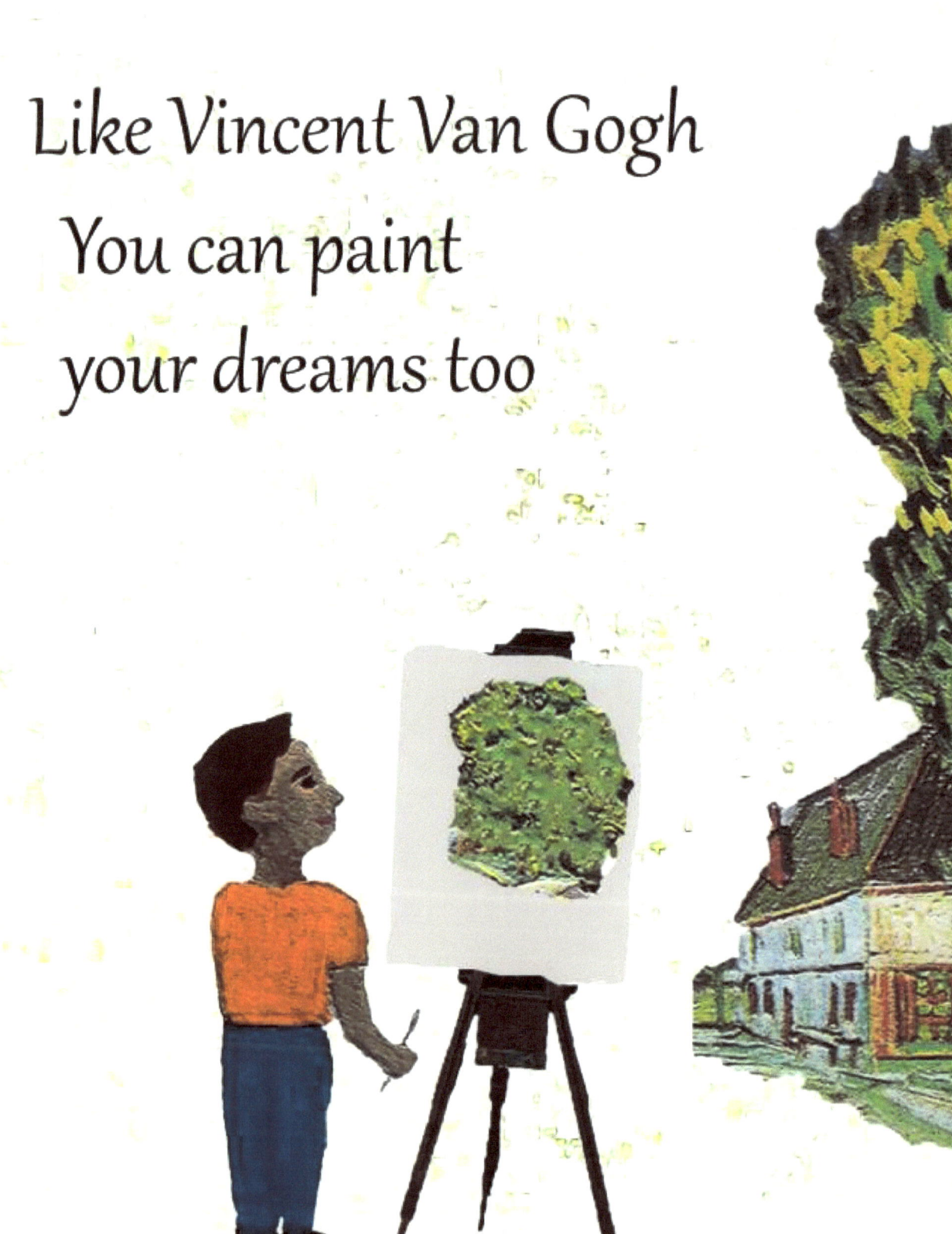

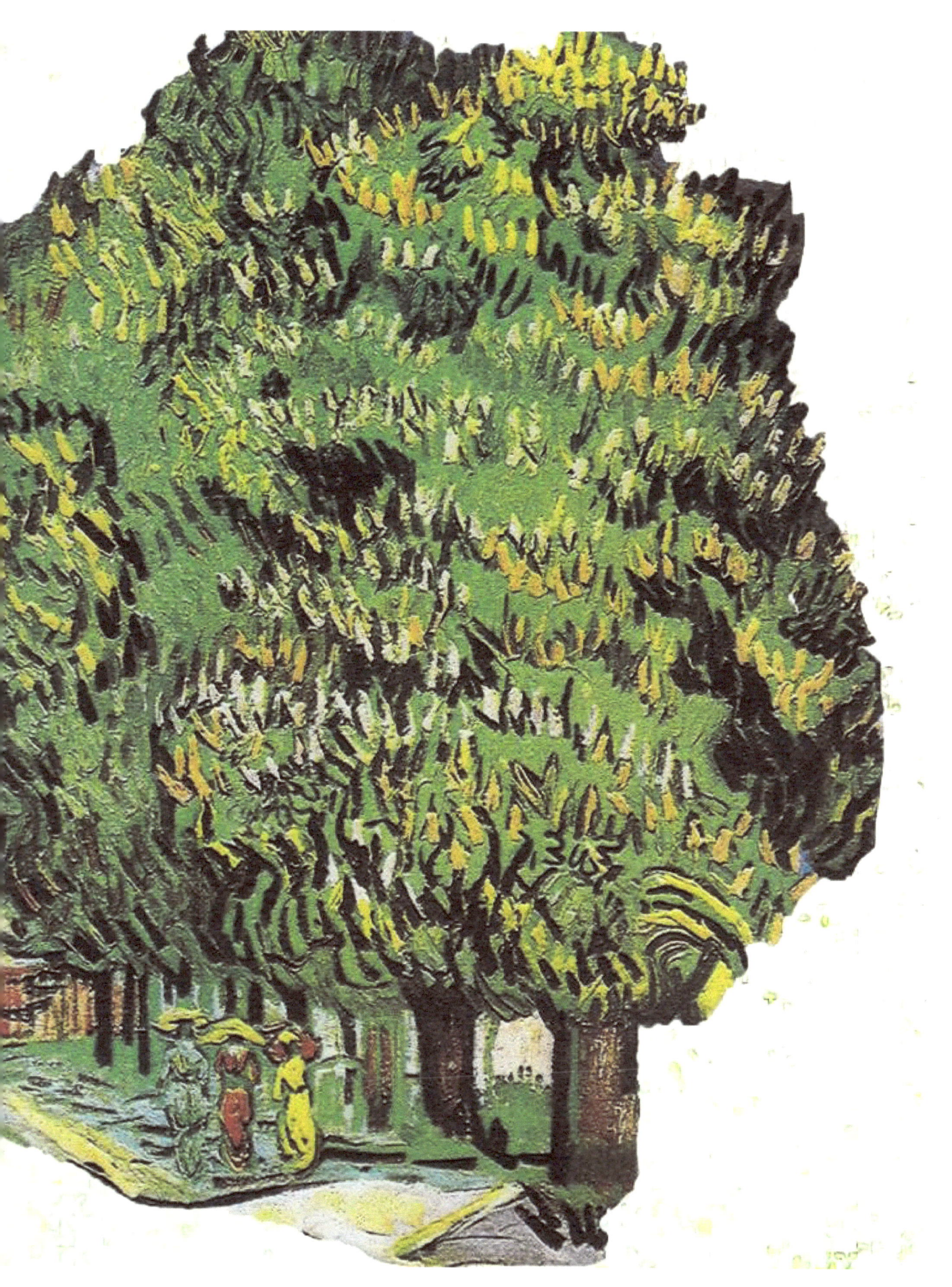

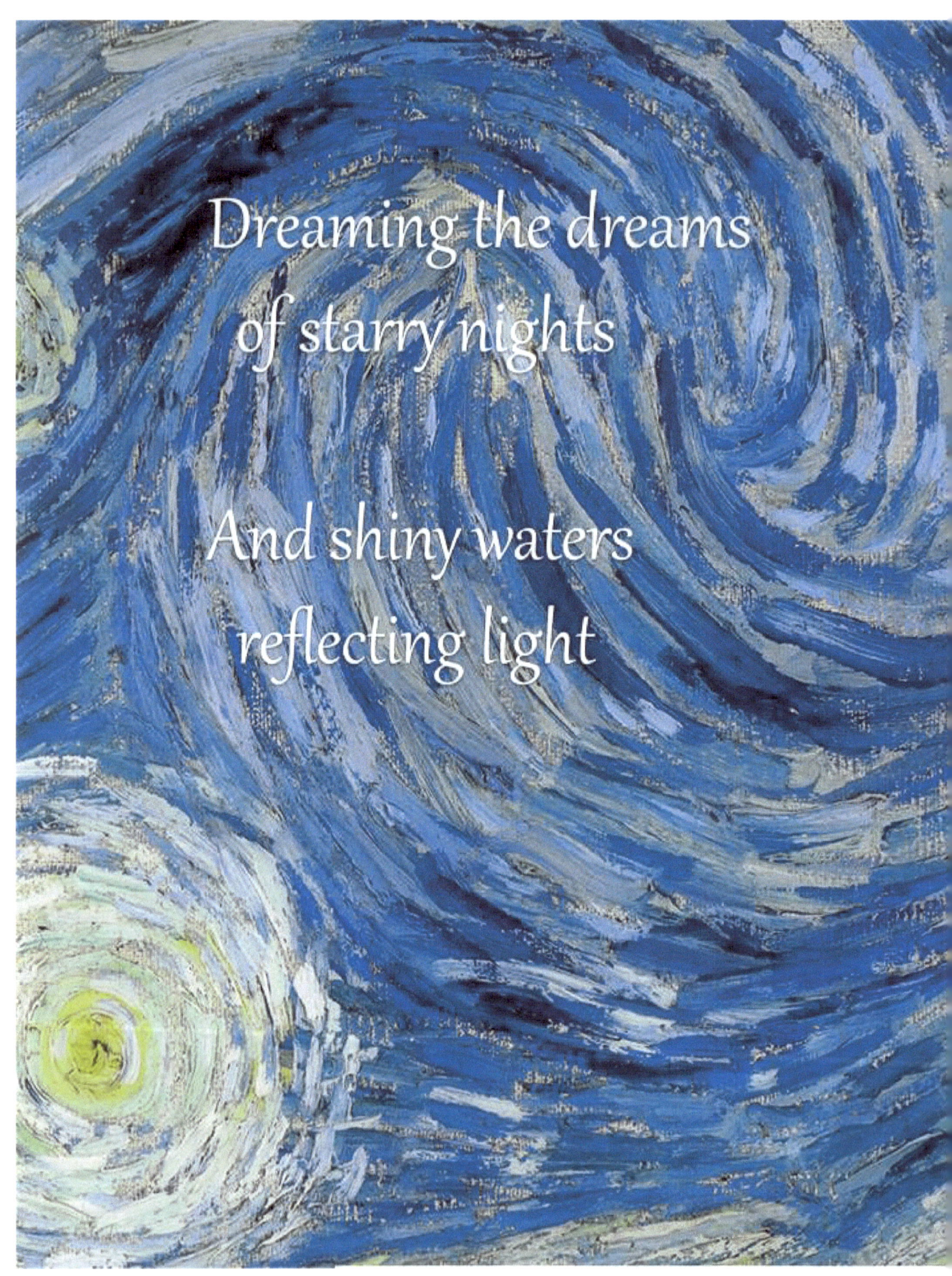

Dreaming the dreams
of starry nights

And shiny waters
reflecting light

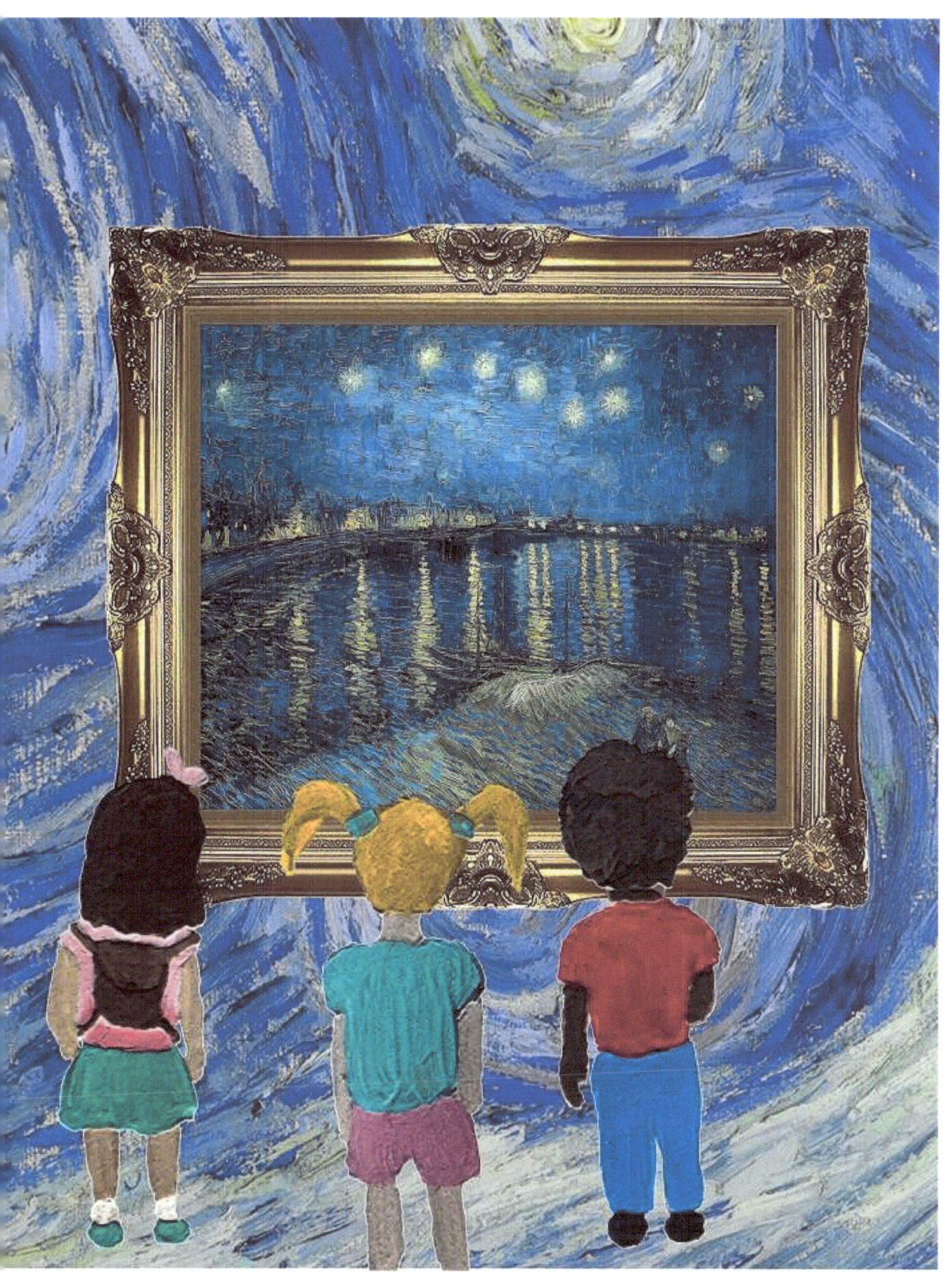

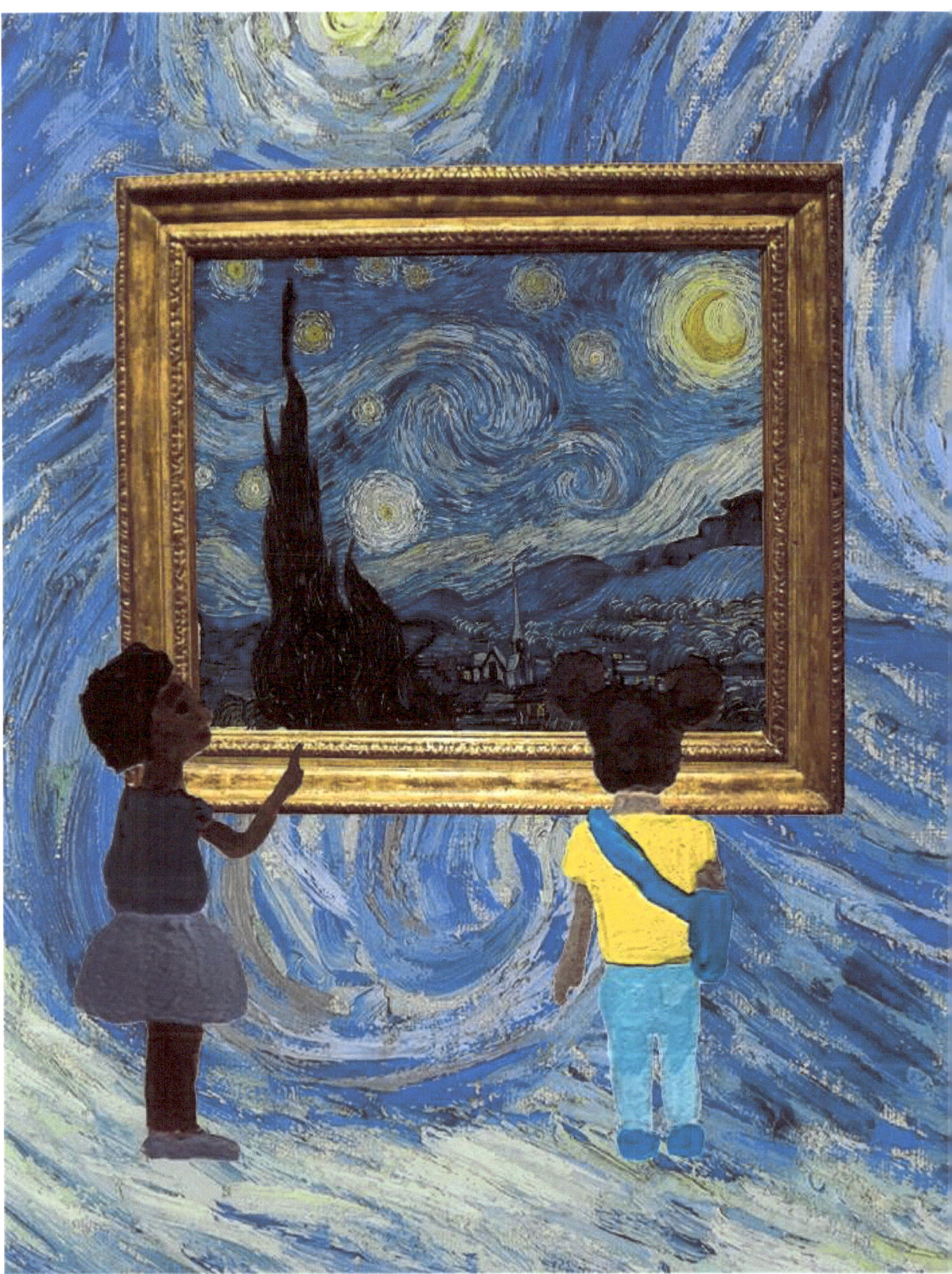

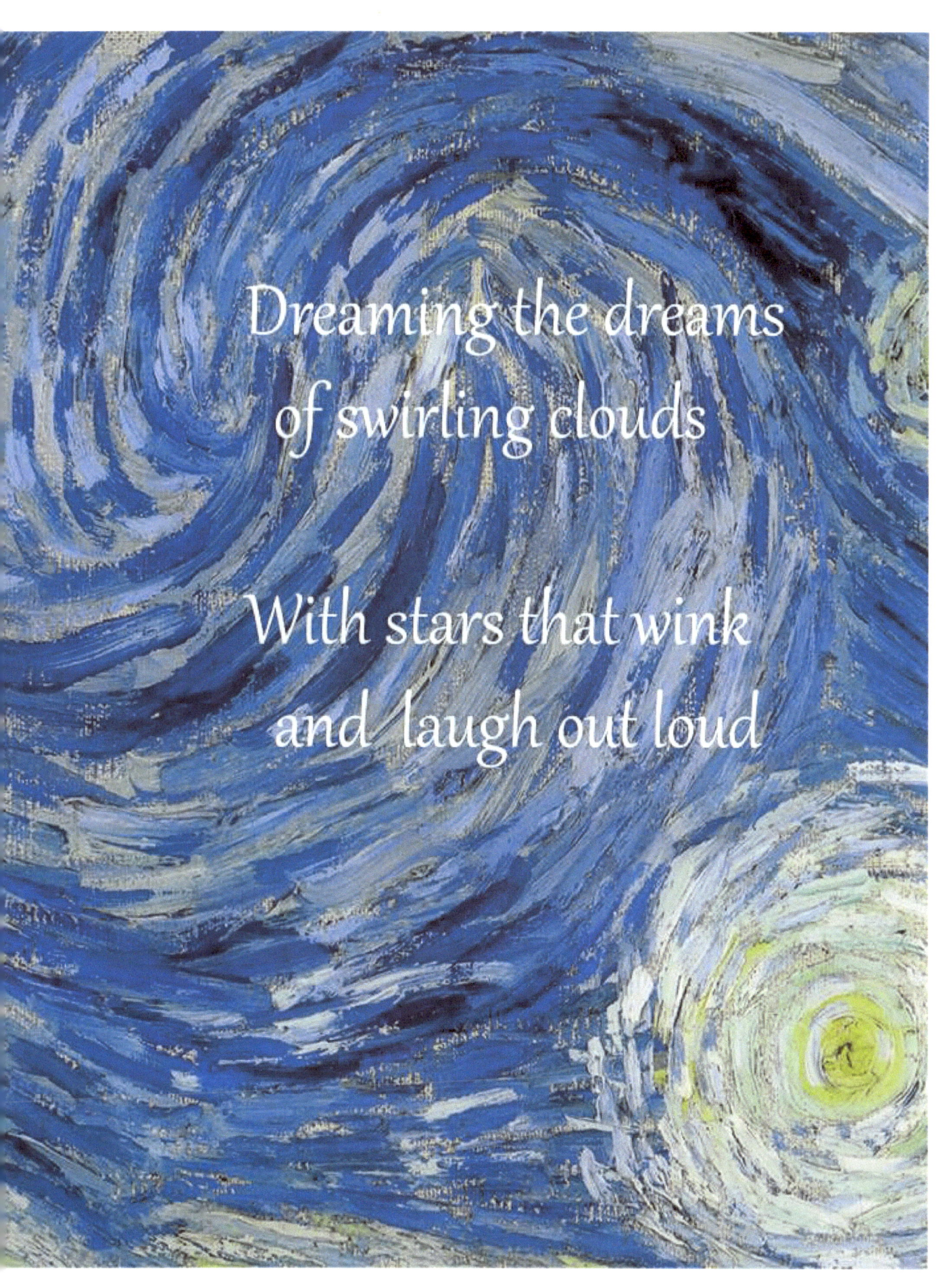

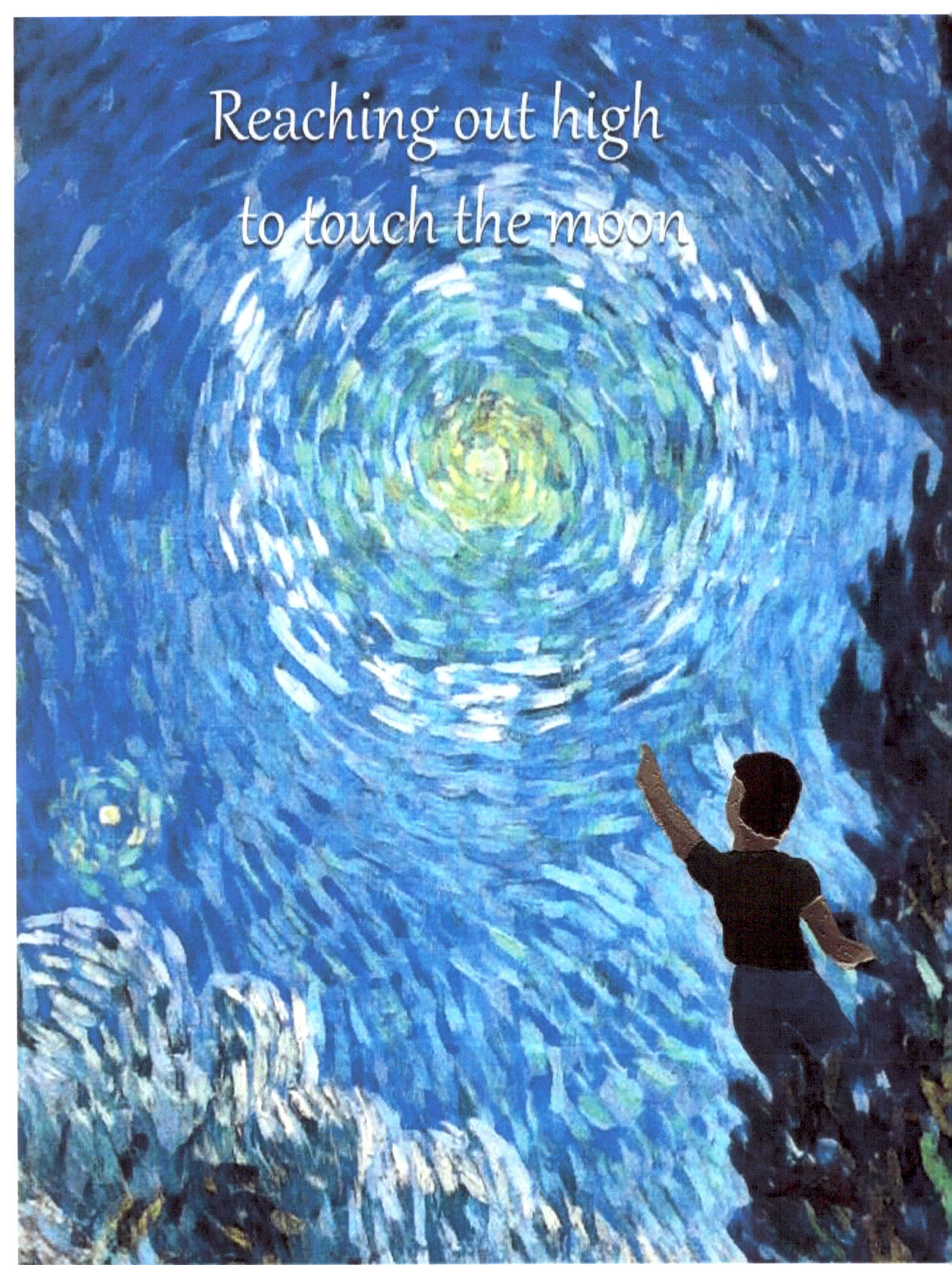

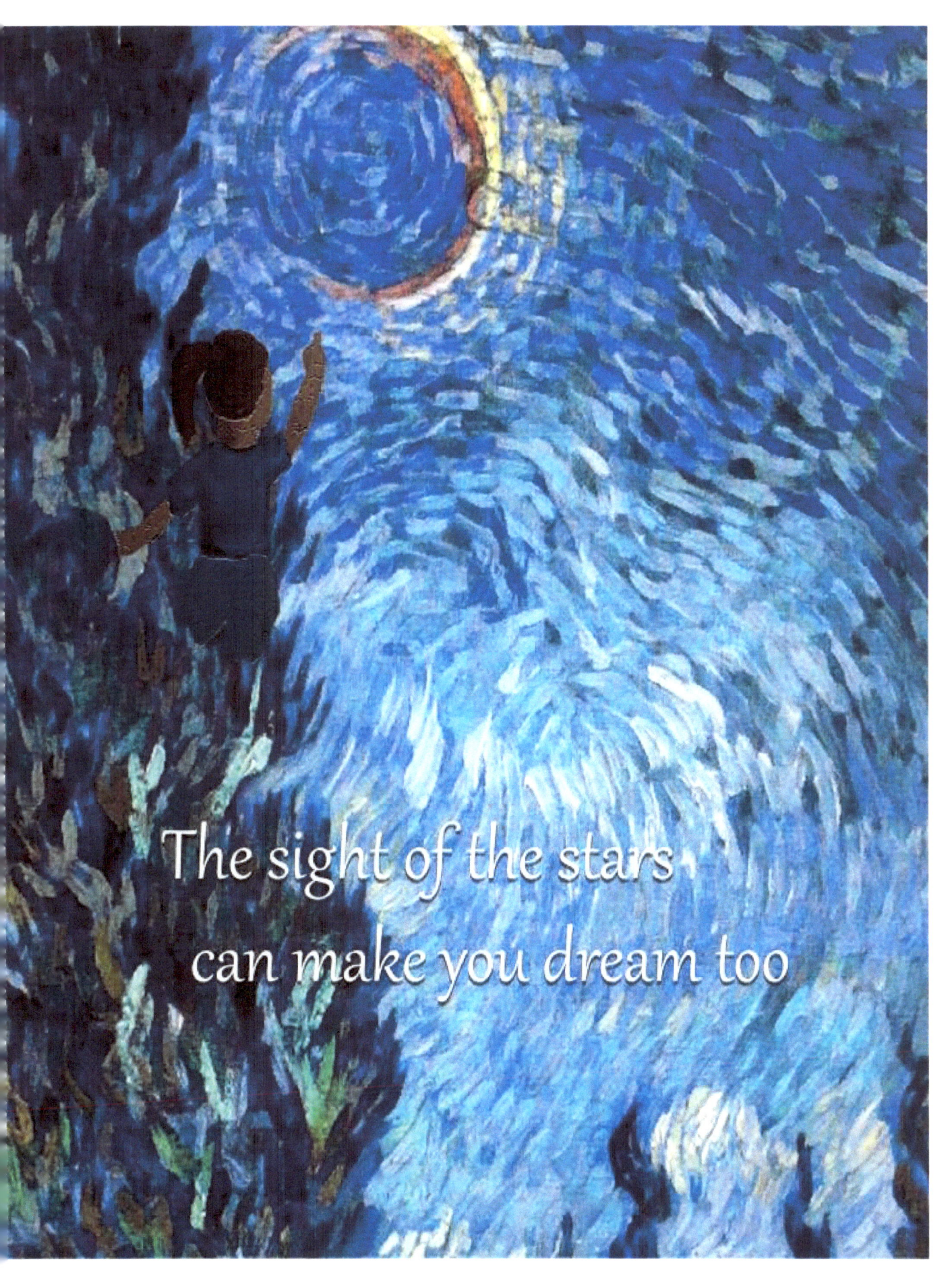

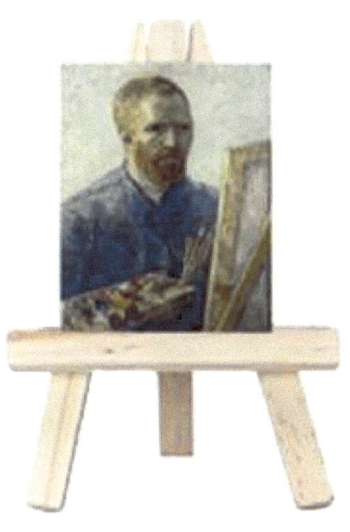

Thank you Vincent van Gogh
for painting your dreams

Vincent's paintings (one to six)

1. Starry Night Over the Rhone – 1888

2. Cafe Terrace at Night – 1888

3. Starry Night – 1889

4. Noon: Rest from Work – 1890

5. View of Saintes-Maries – 1888

6. Wheat Field Under Clouded Skies – 1890

Vincent's paintings (seven to twelve)

7. Sea at Les Saints-Maries-de-la-Mer – 1888

8. Road with Cypress and Star – 1890

9. Falling Autumn Leaves – 1888

10. Bedroom in Arles – 1889

11. Half Figure of an Angel – 1889

12. Chestnut Trees in Blossom - 1890

www.ingramcontent.com/pod-product-compliance
Lightning Source LLC
Chambersburg PA
CBHW051215220526
45473CB00003B/1042